Churches **in trouble?**

Developing good
relationships in your church

Paul E. Brown

Series Editor: Andrew Anderson

DayOne
in association with **FIEC**

© Day One Publications 1999
First printed 1999

Most scripture quotations are from The New International Version.
Copyright © 1973, 1978, 1984 International Bible Society.
Published by Hodder and Stoughton.

British Library Cataloguing in Publication Data available
ISBN 0 902548 92 1

Published by Day One Publications
3 Epsom Business Park, Kiln Lane, Epsom, Surrey KT17 1JF.
01372 728 300 FAX 01372 722 400
e-mail address: sales@dayone.co.uk

Web Site address:www.dayone.co.uk

All rights reserved

No part of this publication may be reproduced, or stored in a retrieval system, or
transmitted, in any form or by any means, mechanical, electronic, photocopying,
recording or otherwise, without the prior permission of Day One Publications.

Designed by Steve Devane and printed by Clifford Frost Ltd, Wimbledon SW19 2SE

Acknowledgements

The ideas expressed in this book have been germinating for many years, and it is impossible to quantify my indebtedness to many Christian friends and colleagues over this period. I am grateful to God for the five and a half years I spent assisting David Fountain at Spring Road Evangelical Church; for the twenty-eight years of ministry at Bethel Evangelical Church where I learned so much through inter-action with many Christian people; and for the four years I have spent at Dunstable Baptist Church. I have been impelled to continue this book to its completion by the many troubles and tragedies I have witnessed all around in the churches of Jesus Christ. The book began with an outline for a booklet by Beverley Savage. I am sorry it has taken so long for his idea to be turned into reality. I am grateful for the urging of Brian Edwards and the Theological Committee of the Fellowship of Independent Evangelical Churches. I thank my wife, Mary, for her support and encouragement. In particular I thank Ron Shipton, my fellow elder at Dunstable, for his comments; Gary Brady, pastor of Child's Hill Baptist Church and editor of 'Grace' magazine, for reading and commenting on the MSS at a very busy time; and Andrew Anderson for his editorial help and encouragement. I take no credit for bringing to view principles which God has already put in his Word, but the responsibility for all mistakes and blemishes is mine alone.

Contents

Introduction

The Lord Jesus Christ intends that those who receive the gospel and believe in him should belong with other believers in churches. In some unusual circumstances this is not possible, but Matthew 18:15-17 shows that Jesus expected that his disciples would normally be joined together in church fellowship. The first church at Jerusalem was one which overflowed with joy and gladness in the early days; there was a great sense of unity and love for one another (Acts 2:40-47; 4:32-37). Since that time many churches have started off like that: as numbers of people have received forgiveness of sins and have come together to worship God, to hear his Word and bear witness together to the gospel, there has been a great sense of joy and heaven has almost seemed to have begun on earth! But things have not usually continued like that. What happened in the New Testament has happened again and again. And it still happens. Problems arise; difficulties have to be faced; temptations seem very powerful; relationships get strained. The joy begins to ebb away and unity becomes increasingly threatened.

The Lord also intends that each church should have its leaders. The New Testament describes a number of leadership roles, and churches today have leaders fulfilling a variety of functions, though the names given to them may differ from church to church. Precisely what leaders there should be and what their exact responsibilities are, does not matter at this point. Leaders are the gift of the ascended Lord (Ephesians 4:7-12). They are given for the good of the churches. They are given to build them up, to care for the members, to exercise wise and loving guidance, to preach and teach the Word of God. An Old Testament verse says, 'When leaders lead in Israel, when the people willingly offer themselves, Bless the Lord!' (Judges 5:2, NKJV). We might paraphrase in New Testament terms, 'When leaders lead in the churches, and when the people willingly follow in the ways of the Lord; praise the Lord!' Many churches have rejoiced greatly at the appointment of leaders; many leaders have proved to be the great blessing Christ intended them to be. But it isn't always like that.

Leadership is a great privilege but it carries great responsibility too. It has its own difficulties and heartaches and can sometimes be a most harrowing and lonely experience. Some leaders have suffered greatly, being stretched to breaking-point and beyond by the pressures put upon them. Equally leadership exercised in unbiblical and unspiritual ways can inflict great harm upon a church and its members. When leaders become tyrants, churches can be fragmented and members can receive wounds which may remain for many years.

From New Testament times onward, churches have experienced the pain and devastation of broken relationships and disunity; sometimes among leaders, sometimes between leaders and members, sometimes among members—and sometimes between them all together! It appears that this is particularly so as we approach turn of the millennium. Yet if the distinctive mark of disciples of Jesus Christ is love, and if a church is a fellowship of those who believe and follow him, then this is tragically and terribly wrong. It is true of course that churches are made up of sinners—saved, but still far from perfect—so that tensions and difficulties are bound to arise. They always will this side of heaven. But while that may explain, it cannot excuse situations which bring great dishonour on the name of Christ.

This book is an attempt to explore from a biblical perspective leadership and relationships within the local church. While written from within the context of independent churches and concentrating upon the local church it is hoped it will prove useful to all varieties of evangelical churches. It is not written out of personal bitter experience; by the grace of God the experience of the author has been to a remarkable degree quite the reverse. It is written out of deep concern to promote the welfare and harmony of churches so that they might glorify God and be faithful, shining lights in the world.

Part 1

Harmony within the local Church

Several other words would be suitable for the heading to this section. 'Peace', 'love', 'fellowship' or 'unity' could all be used instead of harmony, but though each of these is biblical none of them seems to have quite such a breadth of meaning. Of course, 'harmony' will conjure up different audio-visual images for different people. Some will think of an orchestra, perhaps with seventy or so instruments each played by a different person, all making their own particular contribution and blending together to create a unified sound with breadth and depth. Others will think of a choir. Many voices singing together as one; different parts, perhaps with a soloist rising over all the rest, and all combining to produce one effect of beauty. Some will think of a beautiful and melodious piece of music made by an instrument like the piano or organ.

The word 'harmony' when applied to a church conveys the idea of the many members, with their different gifts and abilities, and their distinctive contributions, worshipping and working together; their service together and mutual love and individual participation blending into a psalm of praise for the glory of God. The root of the word is actually found in the Bible, in Ephesians 2:21 and 4:16 where the word 'joined together' is used, first of the building, then of the body. When all the joints (harmoi) are called together in united action there is harmony.

What do we really mean by the harmony of the church? The New Testament indicates that there are a number of different elements which, brought together, constitute harmony. The first of these is love among believers. It is scarcely necessary to demonstrate this. 1 Corinthians 13 is sufficiently well-known to refer to it without quoting. Amongst Christians love is paramount. The greatest gifts and the costliest service are nothing without love. Love is always necessary, always relevant. Among the graces, love is the greatest.

Love expresses itself in fellowship, which has sharing at its heart. All Christians have fellowship with each other because they share a common experience of conversion, they share a common faith in the same Saviour and Lord. They have a common access to the same Father, a common purpose and destiny. This fellowship is expressed practically and developed as Christians meet together and share with each other their various experiences, their understanding of Scripture, their joys, their struggles and difficulties. In this way they can encourage each other, sympathise with each other, learn from each other, strengthen each other.

Fellowship is more than this, however. It is also expressed as Christians worship and work together. To share in praise and prayer, to share in Christian service, to feel part of a worshipping congregation and a working team for the glory of God and the spread of the gospel lies at the heart of fellowship.

Working together contributes to the harmony of the church. The picture of the body is used several times in the New Testament to describe the church. A body is one, but has many parts—arms, legs, hands, fingers and so on; so also the church, it is a unit made up of many members. Just as the parts of the body have their particular place and distinctive function, so do the members of the church. When the parts of the body are all healthy and co-ordinated and working together the body functions properly as a body should. And when the members of the church are spiritually healthy, co-ordinated and function together there is harmony. Sometimes a human body is not properly co-ordinated; some parts go into spasm, arms jerk or eyes twitch, and other parts are not able to obey the directives of the brain. This is a very sad condition, but it is not nearly so tragic, nor even perhaps so common, as a very similar affliction in a church. At its worst a church may tear itself into pieces to the anguish of the members, the confusion of onlookers, and the great dishonour of its Head. However the harmony of a church is beautiful and God-glorifying.

Another element which goes to make up a harmonious church is recognition of leadership. This book is all about the relationship between leaders and members within the church, and if we are going to speak of what makes for harmony we must include respect on the part of members for those appointed to leadership; and also, of course, the exercise of a spiritually-minded, sensitive leadership on the part of those in leadership positions. The Bible mentions this specifically in 1 Thessalonians 5:12,13,

'Now we ask you, brothers (the word includes 'sisters' in its meaning), to respect those who work hard among you, who are over you in the Lord and who admonish you. Hold them in the highest regard in love because of their work. Live in peace with each other.' There also needs to be harmony within the leadership itself.

This may seem idealistic—though it is the ideal we are considering: will not sin spoil the harmony in any church? Inevitably there will be sins within a church; the distinctive thing however about Christians is not that they never sin, but that when they do they know what they must do next. Harmony and love is maintained within a church not by sinless perfection but by repentance and forgiveness. This is something which unfortunately many of us find very hard, and many problems and difficulties have their root more in unwillingness to confess and unwillingness to forgive, than in the actual sins which we commit against each other. The Bible is very insistent about the necessity of a forgiving spirit, 'Be kind and compassionate to one another, forgiving each other, just as in Christ God forgave you' (Ephesians 4:32).

So harmony is a blend of all these ingredients; love, fellowship, working together, respect for leadership and mutual forgiveness.

Just one final word of introduction to this section. Why restrict our thinking about harmony just to the local church? Shouldn't there be harmony between Christians from various churches, and shouldn't churches live and work together in peace and harmony with each other? These questions are, of course, just as important, but there are limits to what one book can tackle so this book will focus on the local church. And there is value in doing this. After all it is when we're thrown into close contact with people; have to cope with their foibles and take their convictions and sensitivities into account, and work together with those we haven't chosen to work with but whom God has brought along with us into the fellowship of a particular church; it is then that grace is tested, and love is called upon, and harmony becomes precious and glorious.

The Work of God

Churches are not human inventions. It is not just that Christians have felt it helpful to get together in groups or assemblies and so the practice of belonging to churches has grown up. When Paul writes to the church at Thessalonica (possibly the earliest of the New Testament documents) he says, 'To the church of the Thessalonians in God the Father and the Lord Jesus Christ' (verse 1 of 1 and 2 Thessalonians). The letters to the church in Corinth both begin like this, 'To the church of God in Corinth.' It is God's purpose that his people should belong to churches so it is right that the first chapter should consider the work of God in the past and present.

WHAT GOD HAS DONE

God has saved us out of the world with its broken relationships and many divisions

When Adam and Eve first disobeyed God the immediate effect was that division was introduced. First and foremost their relationship with God himself was broken: their communion with him was ended. They became afraid of him and when he came to meet with them they hid themselves in the garden. But their relationship with each other was also spoiled. Adam blamed Eve for taking the fruit and giving some of it to him. Eve was told that she would come under the domination of her husband; natural headship would become oppressive rule. Even the relationship between human beings and their environment suffered. Adam and Eve were cast out of the garden and the ground became hostile so that only by labour and sweat would Adam be able to eke out an existence from its resources. These effects are still to be seen everywhere.

When we read the New Testament we find rifts and divisions in society. First of all there was the basic division into Jew and Gentile and this was not merely a national and cultural division. The Jews despised the Gentiles and the Gentiles hated the Jews. Even in the land of Israel itself there was division between Jew and Samaritan, neither having anything more to do with each other than they needed to. The Gentile world was also divided. There was the division between Greek and Barbarian: the Greeks were cultured, intellectual, artistic, but the Barbarians couldn't even speak properly! A far greater division than that was the social division between those who were slaves and those who were free. Slavery in the ancient world was by no means as evil an institution as it became at the height of the slave trade in the eighteenth century, but it was inevitably a great source of antipathy and social unrest.

Sin has brought division, hatred, suspicion, bitterness and a host of other evils that plague the world and bring great unhappiness. Human beings made in the image of God, instead of living together in harmony and reflecting all the characteristics of his goodness, are caught up in the consequences of the fall and their own continuing disobedience to God's Word. As Titus 3:3 expresses it, 'We lived in malice and envy, being hated and hating one another.' But God has done something about this sad state of affairs, and he is still doing something about it. Through his Son he is bringing into being a new humanity, a people whom he will cleanse and thoroughly renew, whom he will perfect and glorify and whom he will place in a new earth where he too will dwell and where all will be righteous. What he is doing, then, is calling people out of the world, out of the dominion of Satan, out of the old life and the old ways, and having forgiven them he is making them the sort of people who will be fit for the destiny he has prepared for them.

God has made us his people

God has, however, done much more than call those of us who are Christians out of the world and the old life. Positively he has made us his people; we were not the people of God, but now, by his grace, we are the people of God (1 Peter 2:10). In the Old Testament God chose Israel; made her his own, delivered her from Egypt, entered into a covenant with her, gave his law and the tabernacle as a place of worship and forgiveness to her. Israel was intended to live a life that was different from the nations around, a life that reflected the glory of God; a life that expressed the fact that Israel was the congregation of the Lord; a life of harmony and peace as the laws of God were obeyed and all fulfilled their responsibilities towards God and each other. In practice, of course, it didn't work out like that, but there is enough in the Old Testament for us to capture a glimpse of a society in which people live as God intended.

In the New Testament the Jewish remnant who received Jesus as Messiah and believing Gentiles make up together the new Israel, the new people of God, the congregation of the Lord (1 Peter 2:9). Christians are his people; now we are to learn how to live out what we are by his grace.

There are three other models that are used to describe Christians in relationship to each other and to God. The first of these is the family. We have been given the right to become children of God, we have been adopted into the family of God. God is our Father, and we are all brothers and sisters. One of the most characteristic ways in which Christians address other Christians in the New Testament is as 'brothers', 'brothers and sisters'. Now if we are the family of God, that will affect our relationships with each other greatly. The local church is made up of brothers and sisters, it is like a little family of God, a household of the children of God. We know that rows sometimes take place within families, but we also know that most families have a sense of identity, of loyalty, and mutual love. Sometimes more family spirit seems to be evidenced among families of unconverted people, than among local families of the sons and daughters of the living God. It is a shameful thing when this is so.

A second model, or picture, that is used in the New Testament is that of a house of God, or temple (1 Corinthians 3:9-17; Ephesians 2:20-22; 1 Peter 2:4-6). Peter describes Christians as 'living stones' which are all being built together to form a house for God to dwell in and where his praises will be sounded out. For a building to be erected all the stones must be fashioned so that they fit together. Awkward knobs and sharp projections have to be chiselled so that a stone is suitable for building into the walls. Not that the stones used in a building have to be all the same size or shape, or exactly regular. There is room for great diversity, but they do have to fit into their place smoothly. This is what makes a building made out of stone, as opposed to brick, so attractive. Ancient buildings where the stones are not held together by mortar but by the exactness of the fit of the stones, are a picture to us of what a local church ought to be like. However such a building cannot be achieved without very careful preparation of the stones and much use of chisel and file.

The third New Testament model is that of the body. Consider 1 Corinthians 12:27. Probably the best translation of this would be, 'You are Christ's body....' (though this does rather throw more emphasis on the word 'Christ' than seems warranted), but it is also possible to read, 'You are a body of Christ...' There seems to be little doubt that Paul is here thinking of the church at Corinth. The local church is the manifestation of the body of Christ in Corinth and it is therefore in the local church that the reality of the body is to be expressed. It is there that the parts are all to find their place, live together and work in harmony. The expression 'the body of Christ' is far too often used in a vague and generalised way. Professing Christians with no commitment to any local church at all drift from church to church on a sea of sentiment, in the supposed interests of the wider unity of the body of Christ. But believers who do not actually belong to a local body of Christians are simply spare parts, detached limbs and members that have opted out of the discipline of corporate life and service. Whatever the difficulties and problems that sometimes arise in local church life, and sometimes these understandably cause disillusion if not despair—the New Testament churches themselves were far from being the models of the perfection some always look for but never find—in the New Testament to be a Christian was to be a member of a local church, and to be out of a church was to be back in the territory ruled by Satan (see 1 Corinthians 5:5).

God has united us to Jesus Christ

This truth is everywhere present in the New Testament, but finds particular expression in the writings of Paul. Christians are 'in Christ'. This has its origin in the electing love of God, believers are chosen in Christ before the foundation of the world (Ephesians 1:4). The call of God is 'into fellowship with his Son Jesus Christ our Lord' (1 Corinthians 1:9). Faith unites us to Jesus Christ! This is the very heart and essence of the unity which Christians have; 'all one in Christ Jesus' is much more than a slogan, it is a fundamental reality.

Being united to Jesus Christ inevitably unites Christians to each other. Moreover the closer Christians draw to Jesus Christ in faith the closer they will be drawn to each other. Real Christian unity and harmony does not arise from things like similar worship patterns, rather it is love to Christ, faith in Christ, and oneness with Christ which draws believers together. This is not an imposed unity, it is an impelled unity. Lovers of Jesus Christ share a common bond, their hearts beat with the same emotion, they understand each other. Though in many ways their experiences have differed yet they have all felt their total need of Christ as Saviour, they are all completely indebted to his grace, their hearts have all been warmed by his love, they all submit to his gracious lordship.

It is against this background that we must understand the horrified question of Paul in 1 Corinthians 1:13, 'Is Christ divided?' The divisions and cliques at Corinth suggested an appalling state of affairs. It was as if Christ himself were being divided, for those who had been 'sanctified in Christ Jesus', 'who call on the name of our Lord Jesus' (v.2), who had all received 'his grace given... in Christ Jesus' (v.4), were fragmented into groups as if they each had their own separate Lord Jesus around whom they clustered. It is not surprising that Paul wrote, 'I appeal to you, brothers, in the name of our Lord Jesus Christ, that all of you agree with one another so that there may be no divisions among you and that you may be perfectly united in mind and thought' (v.10).

God has given us the Spirit

At conversion the believer receives the promised gift of the Spirit, John 7:39; 14:16,17; Acts 2:38,39; 5:32; 15:7,8; Galatians 3:2; 2 Corinthians 1:21,22. This affects the harmony and unity of believers for we have all received and are all indwelt by the same Spirit. This creates what Paul calls 'the unity of the Spirit' (Ephesians 4:3). The Christian benediction in 2 Corinthians 13:14 includes 'the fellowship (or communion) of the Holy Spirit'. There has been much discussion about the exact translation and meaning of this. Is it participation in the Holy Spirit, or is it fellowship created by the Holy Spirit? Even if it is the former it is joint participation in the Spirit, something that Christians share in common. A continuing and deepening of this participation naturally leads to a closer fellowship.

There is a great uniting force in the fact that all believers are indwelt by the same Spirit. The word 'spirit' in general usage often has the meaning of an inner attitude which can be shared by a group of people, 'they share the same spirit'. The idea comes out especially in the French phrase '*esprit de corps'*, the spirit that animates and holds together a group of people. Similarly we talk about 'team spirit'. In a much higher sense, because all Christians share the same Spirit they possess a common mind and attitude which ought to lead to harmony in their relationships with each other.

Moreover the Spirit is the Spirit of adoption. If he enables us to cry to God, 'Abba, Father', we ought to expect him also to lead us to recognise and acknowledge those who are our brothers and sisters in the same family and to show them the love that belongs within families. If he is also the Spirit of truth who leads us into all the truth we should expect a growing agreement amongst Christians and a unity of mind, at least when it comes to the fundamental truths of the gospel. If he is the *Holy* Spirit *par excellence* then we should expect him to be sanctifying God's people so that the passions and sins of the old life are being replaced by new desires and qualities of character which lead, among many other things, to harmony.

God has made us heirs of heaven

It is not uncommon for Christians to base the need for harmony and unity now upon the fact that we shall all be together in heaven. Sometimes this argument is used to the exclusion of all other considerations. If we are going to be together in heaven, the argument runs, we should all be together now, whatever our differences over doctrine, even over the gospel itself, as well as over church order. While it is illegitimate to make a deduction from one truth and use it to over-ride all other biblical considerations, it is a vital truth that all believers are destined for heaven, and that there our unity and harmony will be perfect. We are citizens of the holy city. A city speaks of people in community, people living together, a network of relationships which binds them all together. Certainly this is going to be true of the new Jerusalem. We are inclined to think of any little experience of heaven on earth in terms of individual closeness to Christ, those occasions of deep assurance and joy, perhaps in prayer or the reading of God's Word, which are so precious to us. Without in any way diminishing the blessedness of such experiences, heaven on earth is a more corporate experience than that. We should expect foretastes of heaven much more in the fellowship of God's people than in the secrecy of personal devotion simply because heaven is where we will all be together with the triune God.

WHAT GOD IS DOING

Preparing us for glory by making us holy

We turn now from the past to the present, from what is true of us by virtue of being Christians to what needs to become true of us because we are Christians, from what God has done for us to what he is doing in us and with us. First, because, as we have seen, God has destined us for heaven where we shall share in the glory of his personal presence, he is here and now preparing us for our destiny.

The structure of the first chapter of 1 Peter illustrates this. The early verses of that chapter speak of the living hope that God has given us, the 'inheritance that can never perish, spoil or fade—kept in heaven for you' (vv.3,4). Verse 13 begins a section which has at its heart the call to holiness, 'but just as he who called you is holy, so be holy in all you do, for it is written: "Be holy, because I am holy"' (vv.15,16). Here there is strong link between the hope that we have and the holiness we should seek. The point is much the same as the one made by John, 'Everyone who has this hope in him purifies himself, just as he is pure' (1 John 3:3).

In between the verses we have quoted from Peter there is another thought which is expressed in these words, 'In this [that is, in the final salvation which will be revealed in the last time] you greatly rejoice, though now for a little while you may have had to suffer grief in all kinds of trials. These have come so that your faith—of greater worth than gold, which perishes even though refined by fire—may be proved genuine and may result in praise, glory, and honour when Jesus Christ is revealed' (vv.6,7). Here we see that trials may be necessary—'you may have had to suffer grief'- and that they are purposive; they function to test faith and to purify it. In other words, and this is the perspective which is being emphasised here, God is bringing and using trials of all sorts to make his people ready for the revelation of Jesus Christ and entry into their eternal destiny. God is in control of the lives and circumstances of his people and his concern is to make them holy and thus prepared for the glory which he has for them.

Making us ready to live together as a community

If we need to keep in mind the corporateness of heaven, then we also need to realise that part of the process of being made holy and fit to dwell there will be to make us more able to live together with our fellow believers now. The local church is the place where we are being prepared for the harmony and unity of heaven, it is God's training ground for the community in glory. It is precisely because 'the fellowship of kindred minds is like to that above' that we have to cultivate and develop as far as we possibly can that fellowship now. Notice how Paul speaks of the Colossian church in Colossians 2:5, 'For though I am absent from you in body, I am present with you in spirit and delight to see how orderly you are....' The orderliness of the church, which caused Paul such joy, of course included the organisation and administration, but the basic idea is that everything was in good order. There was harmony, there was a functioning together of all the different members. Relationships between the leaders and members were good and affairs within the church ran smoothly.

Part of our problem, as has been mentioned already, is that we all too easily forget the corporate dimension. We forget that holiness is not just a personal matter, we forget that conformity to Jesus Christ is not just an individual thing but that it works out in our attitudes and relationships with others. It will be a delight to worship and serve the Lord in the fellowship of heaven but it is hard work preparing for that in the local fellowship on earth. There is a little rhyme that goes like this:

To dwell above with saints we love
is going to be glory;
to dwell below with saints we know
is quite a different story!

For all its realism, this has quite the wrong tone for it tends to suggest that going to glory is an escape from at least some of the 'saints below', and that in glory everything is immediately transformed and therefore the best we can do is to put up with each other on earth and wait for heaven! This, however, is just the wrong conclusion to draw. Even now God's people are to aim for unity in the faith and maturity, 'grow[ing] up into him who is the Head, that is, Christ' (Ephesians 4:13,15).

Using church fellowship for this purpose

God uses church fellowship to prepare his people for the unity in heaven. This can be seen from the New Testament in a variety of ways. For example Ephesians 2:11ff. speaks of the Gentiles being brought near to God by the blood of Christ and together with the Jewish believers constituting one body. In the last verses of that chapter Paul says this: 'Consequently, you are no longer foreigners and aliens, but fellow-citizens with God's people and members of God's household ....in him [Christ] the whole building is joined together and rises to become a holy temple in the Lord. And in him you too are being built together to become a dwelling in which God lives by his Spirit.'

Ultimately the holy temple will be completed in glory, then the Church will finally and fully be a habitation of God, but in the meantime Jews and Gentiles have to realise that they are together in the building and must grow up together in unity and harmony. This was not easy, and proved often to be painful in experience. Acts 6 records how the Greek-speaking widows felt they were being unfairly treated and neglected by comparison with the Hebrew-speaking widows. That problem appears to have been fairly easily resolved but tensions between Jews and Gentiles within the Church surface again in Acts 15, and probably lie behind difficulties experienced in the churches at Rome (Romans 14, 15:1-6) and Corinth (1 Corinthians 8 & 10). The point is simply this, that it is in the local church that God brings people from many different backgrounds together. Not just people from different races or cultures, but people from different educational backgrounds, people who are diverse in many ways, people who probably would not otherwise ever meet and might not want to spend time with each other. God brings us all together in our diversity and uses the local fellowship as a means of preparing us for the community of heaven.

Teaching us to live in harmony in all our relationships

We live in a world in which many relationships are fractured and in which tensions and friction are all too common. Part of what God is doing is to make the local church a training ground for restoring relationships. As Christians gradually, painfully and with difficulty, learn to live and to work with each other in the fellowship of the church, so they can begin to put the lessons they learn there into operation in other areas of life and other relationships. Of course it is true that this is often a much harder job, because these other relationships are frequently with unregenerate people, and the grace of God is not operative in them as it is within the church.

It is clear that the New Testament is concerned about how Christians live in their families, and what their relationships are like at work and towards the civic authorities. There are two conflicting principles at work. On the one hand the gospel brings division, (Matthew 10:34f.), yet on the other hand God has called us to peace (Romans 12:18-21). We must never duck the clear words of Christ that the gospel will bring division into relationships; even the closest and most intimate relationships will be affected, indeed they will be especially affected simply because they are so close that the impact of one person within the relationship becoming a believer when others remain unconverted is bound to be felt.

Of course many relationships are already strained before a person becomes a Christian. When a person in that situation is converted some relationships may suffer even more. Nevertheless the believer knows that he is to live at peace, as far as is possible, with everyone. As he discovers within the fellowship of the church the way to relate to others; how to apologise, how to bear with others, so he starts putting this into practice in his relationships outside the church. In this way gradually there will be more harmony in his home or at work, though relationships will only be improved where both sides are willing for it.

God also uses the local church as an example to others. Part of the witness of Christians ought to be the way they get on with one another within the church. Actually that is to put it far too mildly. Jesus said, 'By this all men will know that you are my disciples, if you love one another' (John 13:35). The local church ought to be a very distinctive type of community, one which is impossible for any other group of people. It ought to be one in which the members, however different they may be, nonetheless love each other and worship and work together. There ought to be something about church life and fellowship which can only be explained by the almighty power of the living God who has called its members into fellowship with each other. Then this should spill over into other relationships so that the love, forbearance, sensitivity, concern for others, desire to help, which is found in church relationships is expressed in all other relationships to the glory of God and as a testimony to the world. If only it were more often so!

Fashioning us to make us more useful in his service

According to Ephesians 2:10, 'We are God's workmanship, created in Christ Jesus to do good works, which God prepared in advance for us to do.' God has given us new life and is fashioning us so that we walk in the good works that God intends for us. In order that we might do good works God has given gifts and abilities to all his children (Romans 12:6ff.; 1 Corinthians 12:4ff.; Ephesians 4:7ff.). But these gifts have to be used and developed. While we should beware of thinking of them simply in terms of gifts which are exercised within the church—a very common error in these days, and one which easily leads to a spirit of competitiveness and to people feeling their gifts are overlooked or under-used—yet it is true that many gifts are intended to be used in service within, or at least from, the local church. This means that the use of gifts has to be co-ordinated. It means that we have to take to heart the principle of 1 Corinthians 3:6-8. One plants, another waters; one sows, another reaps; but God gives the increase through the combined operations of two or more of his people. No Christian is supposed to be a Jack-of-all-trades; no Christian is supposed to be a one-man-band. The work of evangelism, the running of the different aspects of the church's ministry, the work of deaconing and care—all these things are usually to be done by Christians with appropriate gifts, abilities and personalities working together.

Moreover the usefulness of all of us is hindered by our sin; by character traits that are harmful, unhelpful, and possibly even repellent. If Christian service is conceived of in a purely individual way it is difficult for these things to be faced and dealt with as they ought to be. We all tend to be defensive and self-justifying when it comes to our own lives. However, when we have to work together with others they are very likely to let us know that they have problems with us—or at least with some of our attitudes and actions. Sometimes this can lead to rather unpleasant situations, but we ought to realise that these arise because of sin—in us, and of course in others also. And it is good for us, and necessary for our growth and development, for these sins and wrong character traits to be brought to our attention so that they can be dealt with. It is very sad to see how some people will only work on their own, or with a very narrow circle of like-minded friends. All too often those who are quirky or awkward in their relationships with others, those who have chips on their shoulders, those with wrong attitudes and unsuspected tendencies to self-centredness, never have these challenged and so remain like this throughout their Christian lives and service. That is a real tragedy.

Using conflicts and troubles in working things together for our spiritual good

It is time to assert boldly what has already been hinted at. The fact is God uses even troubles and personal conflicts in his ongoing work of making us like his Son Jesus Christ. One book which explains this very helpfully is *The Peacemaker* by Ken Sande (Baker). It is subtitled 'A Biblical Guide to Resolving Personal Conflict', and is the sort of book which ought to be recommended and used in every local church. Its first chapter heading is 'Conflict Provides Opportunities.' In speaking about a biblical view of conflict the author first says that some differences which occur between people are neutral and beneficial. He writes, 'Since God has created us as unique individuals, human beings will often have different opinions, convictions, desires, perspectives, and priorities. Many of these differences are not inherently right or wrong; they are simply the result of God-given diversity and personal preferences. When handled properly, disagreements in these areas can stimulate productive dialogue, encourage creativity, promote helpful change, and generally make life more interesting. Therefore, although we should seek unity in our relationships, we should not demand uniformity (see Eph.4:1-13). Instead of avoiding all conflicts or demanding that others always agree with us, we should rejoice in the diversity of God's creation and learn to accept and work with people who simply see things differently than we do (see Rom.15:7; cf. 14:1-13).'

This seems all right, but not all conflicts are like that; some arise out of real sins and hurts. But as Sande goes on to show, we still need to see that conflict provides many opportunities: opportunities to glorify God, to serve others and to grow to be like Christ. 'Conflict is one of the many tools that God can use to help you develop a more Christlike character. To begin with, he may use conflict to remind you of your weaknesses and to encourage you to depend more on him (2 Cor.12:7-12). The more you depend on his wisdom and power, the more you will be imitating the Lord Jesus (Luke 22:41-44). God may also use conflict to uncover sinful attitudes and habits in your life. Conflict is especially effective in breaking down appearances and revealing stubborn pride, a bitter and unforgiving heart, or a critical tongue. When you are squeezed through controversy and these sinful characteristics are brought to the surface, you will have an opportunity to admit their existence and ask for God's help in overcoming them.'

We might as well face the fact that there always will be personal conflicts within local church life. There will be disputes and disagreements about how things should be done. Not everyone will speak with grace and wisdom in the church meeting. People will fall out with each other, and take offence over real or imagined slights. And yet in his extraordinary wisdom God will use all of these in the process of sanctifying us individually and blending and binding the church together as a body of those who serve and glorify him. We all need however to recognise that because of our fallenness these will arise, and though from one point of view they are quite wrong and very regrettable, yet from another they can be remarkably productive in the overall purpose of God for our good. It is our responsibility to humble ourselves and make sure that this is the outcome, rather than division and perpetual strife.

The doctrine of providence

The Bible teaches that every event comes to believers in the providence of God, which means that nothing happens outside of God's control and nothing comes to any believer, or church, outside of God's purpose. There are of course many difficulties with a view like this, but its great benefit is that it leads us to say in any given situation, 'This has come to me in the providence of God; what good does God intend to come out of it?'

This immediately sets us looking at the situation—whatever it is—in a positive way. We all know that if the choice were left to us our lives would be very different from what they are. Things would be so much easier and more pleasant if we had things our way. But we don't; and God plans our lives with mercy and justice (Psalm 101:1), with wisdom, righteousness and goodness.

Events come to us, and come to the church, and at the time we cannot see any purpose to them, in fact sometimes they seem wholly bad and we cannot see any good effects which are likely to follow. However, these things have happened, and they have happened with God, who is sovereign, in control of everything as he works out his all-embracing purpose. Our concern therefore must be to submit to God in what has taken place and to pray and work for good to come out of it. Even sins are taken up and used in the mysterious purpose of God. Situations of utter tragedy when the devil seems to have gained a complete victory are still in the hand of a God who specialises in bringing good out of evil and who is able to make even the wrath of man to praise him (Genesis 50:20; Psalm 76:10).

In some circumstances we are very likely to give way to despair, and both our own hearts and the devil may be encouraging us to this very thing. Yet even if we have sinned personally, perhaps grievously, we can never (if we are Christians at all) be in a position in which God has finished with us and we are simply to give up. Nor, generally speaking, are we ever in a position where the church should give up on us or we should give up on the church. One great tragedy is that when people have sinned they often move off to some other church. Instead of repenting and putting things right within their own church, amongst those who knew the sin and perhaps felt the shame brought to the church and had to cope with the damage, they start again somewhere else. The result of this is that the reality of repentance and reconciliation and the powerful example of the grace of God that these show is not manifested where it needs to be. Similarly, if when there are problems, difficulties and sins within a church, members simply give up and leave, moving to another church which is currently enjoying some growth and blessing, the power of the Word to restore, heal and rebuild is not seen and experienced by those who belonged to it and who should seek the Lord to find his answer to the difficulties. This is not to suggest that it is never legitimate for members to separate from a church; the point here is simply this, if everything comes to us in God's providence, then God has a purpose in all that happens and an answer for every situation.

John Bunyan puts all this pictorially in *The Pilgrim's Progress*: 'After this he [the Interpreter] led them into his garden, where was a great variety of flowers; and he said, Do you see all these? So Christiana said, Yes. Then said he again, Behold, the flowers are divers in stature, in quality, and colour, and smell, and virtue; and some are better than some; also where the gardener has set them, there they stand, and quarrel not with one another.' Where the 'Gardener' has set us, there we are to stand, and quarrel not with one another!

QUESTIONS FOR STUDY AND DISCUSSION

1. What aspects of God's salvation make for community and unity among Christians?

2. Should a Christian belong to a church? What in the Bible supports your answer?

3. What positive benefits may come out of tensions and troubles among members of a church?

4. How necessary is fellowship for growth?

5. Case study: How is 1 Corinthians 1:26-31 an antidote to divisions in the church?

The Responsibilities of the Church

Privileges brings responsibilities. God has been very gracious to every Christian and that brings obligations with it. He has brought us into his family and is working out his purposes for us in relationship with one another. Realising what God is doing in the local church we need to consider our own responsibilities.

RESPONSIBILITY IN THE CHURCH

To understand the situation

We have to come to terms with the fact that God has a multiple purpose for putting his people into churches and that the tensions, strains and relational difficulties of belonging and working together in the church are in actual fact all used by him in the fulfilling of his purpose. This is easy to write but it is not easy to accept in practice. Many churches, perhaps especially the smaller ones, tend to be made up of people who all tend to think alike and who generally get on reasonably well with each other. Very often this is what people mean when they extol the depth of fellowship which they say is found in smaller churches and which they feel is absent in larger ones. Now, of course, differences of doctrine and styles of worship may be very significant and we are not in a position, unhappily, where all evangelical believers in an area can easily—or perhaps even rightly—join together in one church. But sometimes we are in danger of setting up ever smaller groups of people, which we call churches, who are brought together by mutual dissatisfaction with every other church and by the mutual attraction of various factors which are certainly less and other than the attraction of Jesus Christ and him crucified. Worse still the process of doing this is sometimes dignified with the title of church planting.

The point must be stressed, the local church is a place where we are brought together and where we grow together. It is never ideal, never perfect, but it is the environment, the training ground, where God is sanctifying his people, where he is fashioning them to live together as his people, preparing them for the perfect harmony of heaven. If we understand that, and come to terms with it, it will help us enormously and create the right atmosphere in the churches themselves.

To maintain the unity of the Spirit
This is the call of Paul in Ephesians 4:3, 'Make every effort to keep the unity of the Spirit through the bond of peace.' Every word is significant: the opening words indicate that this is not easy but requires considerable effort; 'keep' or maintain, reminds us that the basic unity is given already but has to be preserved and worked out in church life; 'unity of the Spirit', shows us again that this is a unity which could not have been brought into being by human effort and which requires the grace and aid of the Holy Spirit if it is going to be maintained; 'bond of peace', explains that unity is expressed by peaceful relations among church members, such peace binding Christians together in real harmony.

The context indicates several things we need to remember if we are to maintain the unity of the Spirit. The first is the calling with which we have been called, (v.1). It is important to be reminded of the high calling which belongs to every Christian and the obligation which it brings upon us to live up to it. Secondly, we are to make sure our attitudes are what they ought to be; humility, gentleness and patience (v.2) are not qualities which most of us find particularly easy. Thirdly, we are to remember our brothers and sisters—'bearing with one another in love'. It is quite easy not to be bothered about the sins and faults of others, especially if we feel that justifies us in living slack and easy-going Christian lives ourselves. But we will bear with each other if we remember that God is at work in their lives, as well as in ours too. We bear with them because we recognise that God bears with them, that he is also moulding them, convicting them about different areas of their lives at different times, and using their varied experiences for their sanctification. We can bear with them if we love them; and love will show us when their faults make it necessary for us to say something. Finally, we are to remember what unites us. It is easy at times to concentrate on the things which divide, and which sometimes seem so large and important, so we need to look carefully at the oneness shared by all true believers: 'There is one body and one Spirit—just as you were called to one hope when you were called—one Lord, one faith, one baptism; one God and Father of all, who is over all and through all and in all' (vv.4,5).

To think in terms of the good of the whole

Many of us are far too prone to think simply in terms of our own personal growth as Christians to the neglect of a concern for the growth of the whole body of the local church. Take for example the words 'edify' and 'edification'. We often use them in an individual way; we find a book or a sermon 'edifying', yet it is quite clear that in the Bible the emphasis is not on personal edification but on building up the church. In 1 Corinthians 14:4, probably the only verse which suggests that edify can be used in a personal way, Paul says, 'He who speaks in a tongue edifies himself, but he who prophesies edifies the church.' It is quite possible that he is here suggesting that a Christian should not be out to 'build up' himself, but even if this is not so the emphasis is quite clear. Verse 12 says, 'Since you are eager to have spiritual gifts, try to excel in gifts that build up the church.'

The very word 'edify' carries with it the picture of a building. The church is a building, 'you are... God's building' (1 Corinthians 3:9). The foundation has been laid but the work of building up the church has to go on, and while ministers of the Word play their part in this, and must take great care how they build (v.10b), it is surely also true that all the members should be concerned for the growth, stability and beauty of the whole structure. Some Christians are far more concerned with what they 'get out' of a church and its services than with what they can contribute to the spiritual welfare of the whole. There is a 'consumerism' about so many. It often starts even before they join a church. They do the rounds of the churches in an area to see if there is one that will give them what they want. The thought of where they can serve and meet a need doesn't seem to enter their heads.

To promote each other's spiritual good

If our responsibility is to promote the good of the whole body, it is also our responsibility to be concerned for each other as members, and especially for those who are in some way weaker in the faith. We need also to be careful in the way we understand this; the line between thinking we are strong and spiritual pride is not easily drawn. Paul is very insistent about our responsibility to each other when speaking about the problem of meats offered to idols in 1 Corinthians. In 1 Corinthians 8:13 he says, 'Therefore, if what I eat causes my brother to fall into sin, I will never eat meat again, so that I will not cause him to fall.' His commitment to the welfare of his brother in the Lord is total. If something quite acceptable to his own conscience is going to harm his brother spiritually then he is going to have nothing to do with it.

Developing his thought in chapter 10 of the same letter he says in v.24, 'Nobody should seek his own good, but the good of others'; and in vv.32,33 he says, 'Do not cause anyone to stumble, whether Jews, or Greeks or the church of God—even as I try to please everybody in every way. For I am not seeking my own good but the good of many, so that they may be saved.' He goes beyond the bounds of the local church in his thought here: attitudes cannot be kept within rigid boundaries. Someone with a loving desire to promote the spiritual welfare of brothers and sisters in Christ will also have a sensitive concern for unconverted people, in order to win them. Conversely those who are harsh and hard in their attitudes to fellow-believers are not usually very interested in reaching out to unconverted people either.

Perhaps the most helpful way to sum this up is to quote the words of Romans 15:1-6, particularly noting the example cited and the end in view; 'We who are strong ought to bear with the failings of the weak, and not to please ourselves. Each of us should please his neighbour for his good, to build him up. For even Christ did not please himself but, as it is written: "The insults of those who insult you have fallen on me." For everything that was written in the past was written to teach us, so that through endurance and the encouragement of the Scriptures we might have hope. May the God who gives endurance and encouragement give you a spirit of unity among yourselves as you follow Christ Jesus, so that with one heart and mouth you may glorify the God and Father of our Lord Jesus Christ.'

To reform the church

One of the less well-known Reformation slogans is *ecclesia semper reformanda,* the church always reforming; yet it says something which is very important. There are two things which need to be kept separate, and yet which are closely linked together. God revives his church by his Spirit; we reform the church according to the Word. Reformation is not revival, but praying for revival does not take away our responsibility to seek and work for ever closer conformity to Scripture. The work of reformation is not just a matter of government or discipline; it is not just a matter of seeking to ensure that the local church follows the scriptural pattern in its leadership, organisation and worship. Attitudes and behaviour patterns are to be increasingly conformed to Scripture. We cannot say that this will lead to revival (though revival is very likely to lead to reformation), but it is likely to lead to spiritual blessing—'How good and pleasant it is when brothers live together in unity!... for there the LORD bestows the blessing, even life for evermore' (Psalm 133). In any case it is always our responsibility to reform ourselves according to Scripture with the help of the Holy Spirit.

WHAT THE WORLD NEEDS TO SEE

We need also to look at harmony within the church from a totally different perspective, that of the world outside the church. It is commonplace for Christians to remind themselves that their lives are lived under the scrutiny of unbelieving people around them. While this is perhaps particularly true of individual Christians—after all most of us work among unbelievers and have unbelieving neighbours—it is also true of the life of the local church. We may think that most people take no notice at all and scarcely seem aware that our churches exist, yet churches do get a reputation in the neigh-bourhood where they are situated. Perhaps more important than that is the circle of people on the fringe of the church; the relatives and friends of its members, the parents of its Sunday school children or youth club members, the wider circle of 'Christian' people in the area which may include people with a wide variety of beliefs and probably a number who have no true saving faith at all (which is why Christian is in inverted commas). What do these people see when they look at the local church? What ought they to see?

The difference the grace of God makes

There should be something different and distinctive about the local church which marks it off from clubs and organisations, and every other group of people. No church is perfect but all its members profess to be recipients of the grace of God and should have given some evidence that this is so. There should be an atmosphere within the church and attitudes among its members which cannot be explained except for the gracious saving and changing power of God. Love, fellowship, peace, a readiness to accept each other, acknowledgement of sin, willingness to forgive, a desire to help, sorrow over failure—these are only some of the qualities which should be seen in a fellowship of God's people. Such things cannot be hid; nor can their absence. A church in which God's grace shines out is likely to be attractive to people who come into contact with it (though we must not be unrealistic, the grace of God also stirs up the antagonism of the unregenerate heart and the New Testament and history both witness clearly to this). Think of the effect which the Thessalonian church had on the whole area around. Paul is able to write, 'And so you became a model to all the believers in Macedonia and Achaia. The Lord's message rang out from you not only in Macedonia and Achaia—your faith in God has become known everywhere. Therefore we do not need to say anything about it, for they themselves report what kind of reception you gave us' (1 Thessalonians 1:7-9).

People brought together from the most diverse of backgrounds

It is one of the glories of the church that it is made up of people from every sort of background and nation. The apostle Paul rejoices in this when he writes, 'There is neither Jew nor Greek, slave nor free, male nor female, for you are all one in Christ Jesus' (Galatians 3:28). It is not that these differences cease to exist entirely, obviously they do not, but 'in Christ', within the fellowship of the church, they do not matter; everyone is accepted as a brother or sister because all are members of the family of God.

The world can understand people of the same background, or the same interest, coming together and forming close friendships, but when it sees the distinctions and differences which cause people to be separate from and even hostile to each other overcome, then it is impressed. Within local churches the poor and the rich, the less educated and the highly educated, the young and the old, those from the indigenous population and those of ethnic background should all be fully accepted, should form one body, one family, and should actually lose sight of these differences because of the spiritual ties that bring them together in Christ. Again this will not be fully worked out or expressed as it ought to be, but there should be such a measure of harmony among the most diverse of people that this cannot be explained in any other way than by the grace of God.

In a divided and fragmented world, where it is sometimes difficult to find acceptance, harmony and love even within the family, this should be a powerful witness. That churches are not more noted for this type of fellowship is to our shame, and reflects very badly on our understanding of the gospel and its implications. We need an urgent re-evaluation of church life at this particular point. Why is it that the people in many churches are so similar in background, taste, interest, etc.? Why do so many churches seem to reflect a middle class make-up? Do people find cultural barriers in our church? We have a great opportunity for witness if we have eyes to see it; the joyful and harmonious community of Christian people in the local church should show the world where barriers are broken down and how unity of mind and heart can be known.

Reconciliation

All Christians should have gained some proficiency at reconciliation. We are people who by the grace of God have been reconciled to him through Jesus Christ; we have a ministry collectively which involves calling on people to be reconciled to God; and we are to practice reconciliation within the fellowship of the church. 'Be kind and compassionate to one another,' says Paul, 'forgiving each other, just as in Christ God forgave you' (Ephesians 4:32).

Unfortunately the word 'reconciliation' is often used in a careless and unbiblical way to mean simply overlooking wrongs and acting as if sin had never been committed. There is a sort of pendulum swing about this; on the one hand attitudes which in effect condone wrong by never confronting it or expecting apology are praised and considered 'Christian', on the other hand those who show them are very often considered 'soft' and are despised as not living in the real world. Against this background the churches are theatres where the realities of firm but loving confrontation, confession, apology, forgiveness and the full restoration of relationships should be visibly played out. Unfortunately this is not always, perhaps not often, the case. Confrontation is either avoided or else it is hard and cold. Apology is half-hearted and qualified, 'I'm sorry but...'. Forgiveness is grudging, 'Well, all right, I'll forgive you...'. The result is the broken relationship is not fully healed and a legacy of bitterness and suspicion lingers on. Yet the world is crying out to see the sort of reconciliation which will lead it to understand what reconciliation with God means. The churches, and their members, have a great responsibility here. Can unbelievers learn what God has done with you in forgiving your sins and reconciling you to himself from the way in which you forgive others and enter into fully restored relations with them again? This is a question which needs to be considered urgently. So often we feel we cannot be fully reconciled because we have been hurt deeply; but we forget that the honour of God and the visible manifestation of what the gospel does, depends on our showing to others the same sort of forgiving grace that God has shown to us.

Purity and love

Christians and churches should show both purity and love in their lives. Churches need to be disciplined and if members fall into sins, or divisions and factions occur in the church, then it is the responsibility of all the members, especially of those who are spiritual (Gal.6:1), and the leadership, to work for the restoration of those who have sinned and for the healing of divisions. Somehow or other, in practice, purity and love have a tendency to become polarised; those who are most keen to promote the purity of the church tend to a hardness of attitude which is inconsistent with love, while those who show a loving attitude tend to overlook sin and be slack about discipline.

This, however, is an unbiblical polarity, and does not do justice to what the Bible means by either purity or love. In 1 John 2:10, 'Whoever loves his brother lives in the light, and there is nothing in him to make him stumble;' there are three things we ought to notice. First of all we are shown that there is no conflict, or even tension, between light (the light of holiness or purity) and love. Quite the reverse; it is the Christian who loves his brother who continues living in the light. To live in the light includes loving our brothers and sisters; to love our brothers and sisters is part of what it means to live in the light. Love desires what is best for a sister; it wants to promote her highest good and her real welfare. Light expresses itself towards a brother as love; purity of heart excludes jealousy, hatred, bitterness, self-interest, all that is left to be felt and expressed towards a brother is love—at least that will be so when our hearts are wholly pure, and the purer they are the more love will dominate in our relationships.

Secondly, because the verse talks about loving a brother it is speaking of something which is particularly expressed within the fellowship of the local church. Verse 7 of the first chapter says, 'But if we walk in the light, as he is in the light, we have fellowship with one another...' and part of the reason for this is now plain, 'walking in the light' includes 'walking in love'. Purity and love going hand in hand are what make for fellowship between brothers and sisters in the church. There is no real fellowship where sins and hurts and divisions fester under the surface of an appearance of love which is achieved by people keeping a measured distance from each other, and only greeting each other with a smiling politeness when they have to. Nor is there any real fellowship where purity of life and order in the church are brought about by fear of one another, or fear of failing to meet the high standards which everyone else, or at least the leadership, seems to have.

In the third place, the last part of this verse is very significant, 'and there is nothing in him to make him stumble'. Doubtless the main thought here is that he who loves his brother does not cause him to stumble. A person who loves gives no cause for stumbling into sin (or division, or error) in the church. This applies beyond the church to the world outside. When churches exude a loveless attitude or when obvious sins and evils are tolerated in them, the world does take offence and is stumbled. Unbelievers cannot stand hypocrisy (at least among Christians!). But walking in light and love gives no cause for the world to criticise.

God is both light and love (1 John 1:5; 4:8,16). At different times in history, one or other of these has received the emphasis and the result has been a serious imbalance. At times the emphasis has been on the fact that God is light. At present the general opinion is that God is love, and this is taken to mean that God probably will not judge anyone, or if he does he is likely to be pretty lenient, and certainly will never send anyone to hell. His law is looked upon as probably all right as a general rule, but it has many exceptions, and to be legalistic is about the biggest sin that anyone could fall into. It is part of the responsibility of churches to correct this false impression, not just by preaching and teaching, but also by the principled love that should motivate and guide conduct and relationships both within the church and towards those outside.

Something new that speaks of heaven

Most people live almost exclusively for the present. Any hopes they may have for a life beyond this one are generally very vague, and as a result such hopes have very little motivating power when it comes to living now. We have already seen that God is preparing believers in their churches for their destiny in heaven. To some extent, then, we should expect something of what it is going to be like in heaven to be seen even here in the fellowship of the church.

Looking at a church the world should be able to see something new that speaks of heaven. This is surely very important, though also extremely challenging. Can we really expect church life to be of such a quality, its relationships of such a spiritual and harmonious nature, that it points an unbelieving and ignorant world to the reality of heaven beyond this life? Every church will show only too obviously that its members belong to this age and are far from having reached the perfection of the age to come. But this should not be the only thing that a church shows; it should also be a mystery that, made up as it is of human beings who at one time were no different from anyone else, it has a quality of relationship that is found nowhere else, one that is a pointer to the perfect society that God is going to bring about in the glory of heaven. Preaching about the perfect future condition of God's people should appear credible when the church's corporate life is seen and the ongoing changes in its members are considered.

In Philippians 3:20 Paul writes, 'But our citizenship is in heaven...' Is there any evidence that this is so? Is there anything someone outside could notice which would lead them to realise that Paul is speaking the truth? If our citizenship is in heaven, surely there ought to be some evidence of the life of heaven within our churches? Consider also the Lord's prayer:

'Hallowed be your name,
Your kingdom come,
Your will be done,
As in heaven so on earth.'

It can be argued that the last clause belongs to all the three petitions above. Where on earth are these petitions at least partially answered; where on earth is God's name hallowed, where has his dominion come, where is his will done, if not among his people and within the churches? Where on earth, then, is what is true of heaven expressed at least to some extent? It must be in the churches and, if it is, it ought to be visible.

CHRIST THE HEAD

Jesus Christ himself is the head of the church. Ultimately harmony comes from him. It is by the grace of Jesus Christ and through submission to his leadership that relationships in the church are harmonious. That Jesus Christ is 'head' is seen in some of the other words and phrases that are used of Jesus Christ in his relationship to his people. The word 'shepherd' is used several times in the New Testament, first of all on the lips of Christ himself, 'I am the good shepherd' (John 10:11,14). The shepherd 'calls his own sheep by name and leads them out' (John 10:3), they 'follow him, because they know his voice'(vv.4,27). Harmony arises from listening to the voice of the shepherd and following him. He does not lead his sheep as individuals, but as a flock; they go in and out together as they listen to his voice and obey. Closely associated to this is the word 'overseer', (1 Peter 2:25) 'the Shepherd and Overseer of your souls'. Christ watches over and cares for the souls of his sheep far more diligently and affectionately than any of his undershepherds (Hebrews 13:20; 1 Peter 5:1-5). He knows how to heal and restore; he knows how to bring his flock together, and how to lead them on in unity.

He is also 'the author' of our salvation (Hebrews 12:2), perhaps here 'leader' or 'captain', or possibly better still 'file-leader', the one who goes before and blazes the trail so that those who come after must follow closely in his footsteps. In Hebrews 3:1 he is the 'apostle', the one like Moses, who was sent by God to lead his people through the wilderness and bring them safely to the land of promise. All these words emphasise the idea of following and obeying. Jesus Christ is head and lord and it is by submission to him in all things that harmony is developed within the churches.

How then does Christ speak to his flock; how is his voice heard and his will known? Christ speaks by his Word and his Spirit. Although it would be possible to consider both of these separately it is better to think of them together, for they belong together. In the Word of God we have everything that we need for the life and obedience of the churches, 'All Scripture is God-breathed, and is useful for teaching, rebuking, correcting and training in righteousness, so that the man of God may be thoroughly equipped for every good work' (2 Timothy 3:16,17). The way to harmony is through submission to Christ by obedience to his Word. Why then the mention of the Spirit of Christ?

First, we cannot fully and spiritually understand the Word of God apart from the Spirit. Paul's prayers give eloquent testimony to his recognition that the churches need wisdom and insight to understand God's will (Ephesians 1:17ff.; Philippians 1:9-11; Colossians 1:9ff.). Not only did Paul write to the churches to explain to them their duty, he also prayed for them that the Spirit might give them the insight and spiritual understanding that they needed. Secondly, while in one sense the whole New Testament, indeed the whole Bible, is always obligatory upon the churches, it needs spiritual insight into the condition of a church to see what is particularly necessary at a particular time for a particular condition. In this sense it is possible to apply the words of chapters 2 and 3 of the book of Revelation, 'He who has an ear, let him hear what the Spirit says to the churches'. In the prophetic letters to churches of Asia there will often be found words of particular importance to one church or another, just as was the case when they were first written and sent both to each church and to all the churches together.

Another way in which the Spirit's ministry is crucial, is in the application of the general principles of the New Testament to the particular situations and problems confronting the churches in these days. We live in very different times and it is not easy to take the principles of the New Testament and apply them to the specifics of life in the twentieth century. For this we need the wisdom and spiritual grace supplied by the Spirit. Furthermore the Spirit enables the churches to obey the Word in a spiritual and evangelical manner. The Word not only speaks about outward actions, but about the motives from which they are to spring, the attitudes which they are to express and the purposes which they are to further. These motives, attitudes and purposes are all spiritual and gracious and cannot be present apart from the working of the Spirit. Bare, outward conformity to the Word is not enough; outward obedience to the Word must be matched by inward submission and delight in it.

At the end of his prayer in Ephesians 3:14ff. Paul writes these remarkable and heart-stirring words, 'to him (God) be glory in the church and in Christ Jesus'. This is finally what this chapter is all about and why harmony is of such supreme importance. Its purpose is glory to God in the church. What could be higher, or greater, than that? In the church; in our churches; in the church to which each of us belongs—glory to God and in Christ Jesus! Many things contribute to glorify God in the church, but not the least of these is harmony. Love, peace, fellowship, working together, mutual submission, recognition of leaders, restoration and reconciliation; all these produce harmony in the church, and glory to God.

QUESTIONS FOR STUDY AND DISCUSSION

1. What areas of church life need continuing reform?

2. Is it realistic to think that people who are very different can all form one worshipping community? What will it take to make this a reality?

3. How are love and sentimentality different?

4. What bearing does holiness have on good relationships?

5. Case study: How does the description of Christ as head in Ephesians 4:15,16 throw light on the earlier part of the chapter?

Part II

Reasons for discord

We have been considering the harmony which ought to exist within the church; looking at the ideal and setting out the goal for which we should be praying and strenuously working. In this chapter we come back to reality—perhaps with a bit of a bump!

It is easy to idealise the early days of Christianity. The growth and spread of the gospel as recorded in Acts was remarkable; who of us would not long for days when 3,000 are converted by one sermon, or to see the Lord adding to the church daily those who are being saved (Acts 2:47)? However, we don't have to go far in Acts to see division and discord arising among the believers.

In Acts 6 we find the Greek-speaking Jews complaining about the Aramaic-speaking Jews because their widows were being neglected in the daily distribution which was made for their needs. Presumably this was not something which was deliberate. It seems to have arisen because the apostles had too much to do. It was remedied by the appointment of seven men, perhaps the first deacons, to handle this ministry. This event illustrates how easily discord can arise. There were already two distinct groups within the church, and this was a potential source of trouble. The apostles were too busy, and were not able to ensure that there was no unfairness in treating the widows. Because there was some unfairness, complaining set in—one dictionary says that the word here is used "generally of smouldering discontent". All very understandable, but not the right way for Christians to respond. Notice that when the matter was righted, 'the word of God spread. The number of disciples in Jerusalem increased rapidly' (Acts 6:7).

The second example is much more surprising and its 'solution' leaves us feeling dissatisfied and disappointed. The church at Antioch seems to have had a spiritually-minded group of leaders and as they ministered to the Lord and fasted the Holy Spirit said, 'Set apart for me Barnabas and Saul for the work to which I have called them' (Acts 13:2). Here is something new in Acts. The apostles had already been called by Christ and commissioned to preach the gospel, but now from within a local church two men are called to go out and engage in missionary endeavour. We can imagine the joy and sense of privilege and anticipation with which the church at Antioch would have sent them out to serve the Lord.

In due time they came back and the church gathered to hear the report of 'all that God had done through them and how he had opened the door of faith to the Gentiles' (14:27). Paul and Barnabas remained with the church for a long time and then went up to Jerusalem to deal with a problem which had arisen between the two churches—another area in which discord can easily arise. On returning to Antioch Paul felt it was time to go back and visit the churches formed in all the towns where they had preached the word of the Lord. However, Barnabas wanted to take John Mark with them again while Paul was insistent that they should not take someone who had left them the first time and not gone on in the work. The result was this, 'They had such a sharp disagreement that they parted company' (Acts 15:39).

It seems almost impossible that these first two missionaries should have had such a disagreement, then that they were unable to work out some sort of compromise or arrangement between them, and finally that they should have actually separated from each other. What effect this had on the church at Antioch we are not told, though as the members there sent out Paul and Silas it seems as if their sympathies were with Paul. We may believe that God over-ruled the separation for good in the end, and used it for the rehabilitation of Mark, but in itself it was clearly a tragic case of discord.

A third example comes in Philippians 4:2. Here Paul urges two women in the church to be of the same mind in the Lord. The general tone of the letter to the church at Philippi is one of joy and the sort of rebuke and correction which Paul found necessary when writing to some other churches is absent. Nevertheless he issues this strong appeal as he draws to the end of what he has to say. This must have been a long-standing and perhaps rather bitter disagreement for it to have been sufficiently serious for Paul to write about in a letter which would have been read out before all the congregation. One wonders whether, if Euodia and Syntyche had known they were going to be immortalised in Holy Scripture, they might not have made some mighty efforts at reconciliation! We can also assume that this disagreement had repercussions beyond their own personal relationships. Doubtless it was well-known and even if the rest of the church had not taken sides it would have cast its shadow over the fellowship of the church and its functioning as a body.

Finally the example of the church at Corinth must be noted. Paul has to do some more appealing, 'I appeal to you, brothers, in the name of our Lord Jesus Christ, that all of you agree with one another so that there may be no divisions among you and that you may be perfectly united in mind and thought. My brothers, some from Chloe's household have informed me that there are quarrels among you' (1 Corinthians 1:10,11). The divisions at Corinth were many and very serious, as the letters to the Corinthians reveal. Here was a situation in which division had become endemic in the church. It was not just that two people had fallen out with each other, or even that there were two factions within the church. Division, quarrelling, backbiting, had become a way of life within the church. This was an utter scandal and a living denial of the harmony that ought to have existed.

From the members themselves

If any group of people ought to be at peace among themselves it should be the members of a church. And if there is any disturbance or trouble in a church surely it must arise from some outside influence. So it might be thought. The truth is, however, that many of the ingredients that make for difficulties within churches arise from the members themselves. So that is where we must start.

GENERAL REASONS

We have the seeds of all sins within ourselves

This is a very humbling truth to realise and face up to, but it is the fact. It is easy enough to see and deplore faults and weaknesses in other people, but the principle of sin, and thus the root of all the whole variety of sins, remains within every Christian. Jeremiah reminds us that 'The heart is deceitful above all things, and beyond cure' (17:9). This is not just the condition of the unconverted; it is part of the corruption of human nature as a result of the fall, and the deceitfulness, unreliability and unpredictability of the human heart is a factor which all Christians have to reckon with. It was because Peter did not know his own heart that he could confidently assert that he would be faithful to the Lord, yet soon after deny him with oaths and curses (Mark 14:29-31,66-72). Not only is the heart deceitful, but sin itself is something deceitful (Hebrews 3:13). For this reason we need to take special care. Sin so easily takes us in. In most disputes, for example, both sides are usually ready to justify themselves. Sin deceives us; it tries to make itself out to be something other than it is; it persuades us that our attitudes are right and good, and it tries to highlight to us the faults and failings of others.

Paul tells us, 'I know that nothing good lives in me, that is, in my sinful nature' (Romans 7:18). Not every Christian, however, seems to possess this knowledge, or at least reckon with it. Self-knowledge, self-distrust, a recognition of our liability to fall, a watchfulness and prayerfulness to try and ensure that we don't, are extremely important in seeking to avoid discord. On the other hand where people are self-confident in their own ability, over-confident about their own judgments and opinions, unaware of the reality and power of indwelling sin, there is likely to be trouble.

We are exposed to the whole range of temptations

All Christians know that we live in a world which presents us with many temptations. We are tempted by the things which we see and hear, and by the example of others. We are tempted to speak, act or live in ways which we perceive as being for our advantage, though they may hurt others. We are tempted to think in terms of our own welfare or advancement rather than the good of the body of believers to which we belong (cf. Philippians 2:4).

It is easy to underestimate the range and power of sin in our own hearts, and it is just as easy to underestimate, if not be almost unaware of, the wide variety of temptations to which we are subject. It was not for nothing that our Lord Jesus taught us to pray, 'And lead us not into temptation.' Many believers are so blind to temptation that it is only the mercy of the Lord in answering that prayer that keeps them from sinning in many more ways than they do.

In considering relationships within the church we have to reckon with the power of temptation. We need to realise that things can go wrong, and watch out for temptation so that they do not go as wrong as they might. The words of our Lord Jesus Christ are sobering indeed, 'Woe to the world because of the things that cause people to sin! Such things must come, but woe to the man through whom they come! If your hand or your foot causes you to sin, cut it off and throw it away.' (Matthew 18:7,8). This warning shows what a serious thing it is to cause other believers to sin, especially the young and immature. To cause others to stumble and upset them spiritually by our selfishness, pride, hamfistedness, and carnality is a great evil which calls for watchfulness and avoiding all known avenues of temp-tation. 'Watch and pray so that you will not fall into temptation' (Matthew 26:41).

We are at all stages of growth and development

Obvious though this is, it is all too frequently overlooked. In nearly all churches there will be a range of age, experience and development. Some will be recent converts; some will come from a non-Christian background; some will have particular problems and difficulties, some will be more mature. To speak in terms which Paul uses some will be weak as believers, others will be strong.

So for church members to grow together and learn to function harmoniously together will not be easy. For them to maintain their individuality and individual contribution while at the same time co-operating with all the other members is not likely to come about without misunderstandings and mutual exasperation! Hopefully, the situation will continue to be even more confused as still more people are added to the church! Some of these may come from other churches, where they did things differently. A church should be a growing, developing body and the pains and tensions of growth must be recognised, even though all the members should play their part in seeking to minimise these as much as possible.

We are in different spiritual conditions at a given time

It would be wonderful to find that when people become Christians they then begin to grow with a steady upward trend. But this is not what happens. Some believers seem to get stunted early on and their growth appears minimal. Some appear to make great progress and then something arises to hinder them, just as it did with the Galatians (see Galatians 5:7). Many grow by fits and starts; often with long periods in which they carry on without very much discernible progress. Not a few fall into disobedience and have periods of backsliding, or at least times when their relationship to the Lord is in a thoroughly unsatisfactory condition.

Such a state of affairs also makes for discord within a church. We have to be realistic; it is often going to be like this. This places a particular responsibility on those with pastoral oversight and ministers of the Word of God. It is as believers are helped to grow that discord is likely to diminish, but also as fellowship and good relationships are developed within the church so believers grow. And those in positions of leadership have to look out for themselves. The same variations in spiritual experience are found within leaders too, and many of the problems that have beset churches have arisen when those in leadership have become complacent or backslidden or proud or hungry for power.

We are from different backgrounds

Acts 6 has already reminded us of the potential for tension when there are members from different backgrounds within a church. We have seen, too, that it is part of the glory of the gospel to bring people of different temperaments, social background, education and nationality together into the one local church. But it is also quite evident that such differences are going to be difficult to handle and there is going to be no quick way to harmony in such circumstances. For this reason it is tempting to feel that the best thing is for a church to be what has been called a 'homogenous unit', a church made up of people who have a natural affinity with each other. This would mean it is best to have middle class churches and working class churches, black churches and white churches and so on. This however is really a denial of what unity in Christ means, and is it not something to aim for. It should rather be a matter of regret if circumstances have brought it about.

NEW MEMBERS AND IMMATURITY

All churches should long and pray for an influx of recent converts from unbelief. Yet when it happens, though it causes praise and thanks to God, it may bring with it considerable upheaval in the life of a church. When converts come from completely ungodly backgrounds they can bring complications and tensions into relationships in the church. Consider the factors operating in these circumstances.

Conversion is only the start of a lifelong process

All conversions have within them the seeds of growth in right living and love for fellow Christians, and in some cases there is a considerable transformation in the character and life of the person converted almost immediately. Growth in grace and knowledge of Jesus Christ, however, is something that goes on throughout the Christian life and often with some difficulty. There are hard lessons to be learnt about oneself; there is a humbling process that has to take place; there are new attitudes to be learnt and developed; love has to be worked out in practical ways that the new convert had never dreamed of prior to becoming a Christian. To start with, all is wonderful in the church; the believers are rejoicing; everything is fresh, new and glorious for the convert, but it is not at all surprising if then problems begin to arise.

Churches, and especially the leadership, should anticipate this. Grace, forbearance, wisdom and patience are required on the part of established Christians. It is sad to see the way in which some older believers react. They seem to think that new believers should adapt almost immediately to their new life and that they should instinctively understand all the procedures and language of the church and fit in like books in a bookcase. When this does not happen sometimes the very reality of the conversion of new believers is called into question. Such an attitude can itself be a serious hindrance to the progress of the convert and only serves to make the whole situation more difficult. Perhaps one of the reasons why the Lord does not add more converts to some churches is because he knows how they would be received if he did.

New converts should be received with love and joy along with an acceptance of their immaturity and a real desire to help and teach them. They should not be patronised, nor should they be made to feel that they are unsettling to the congregation. Right from the beginning they should be valued as members given by the Lord and their gifts should be noted so that they might be encouraged to develop them for the service of God. Not that they should be pushed into activities that they are not ready for and which may be spiritually harmful for them (see 1 Timothy 3:6,7), but they should be encouraged increasingly to play their part in the life of the church.

New believers may bring with them attitudes and hang-ups from their past life

People brought up in a Christian home with a church background unconsciously absorb many Christian attitudes which are of tremendous value to them when they are converted. Those without such a background inevitably have very different standards, values, ways of thinking and reacting. Some Christians seem to think that such ingrained attitudes should be immediately altered upon conversion, but this is not usually so.

Transformation by the renewing of the mind (Romans 12:2) goes on throughout the Christian life.

However it can be very disconcerting when recent believers bring very worldly attitudes into the life of a church, and we must not underestimate the problems that this can cause. The apostle Peter said to the people to whom he sent his first letter, 'We have spent enough of our past lifetime in doing the will of the Gentiles...' and this indicates that he saw the danger of past behaviour intruding into present living. If people have been really born again then they will respond to loving correction and guidance and this is something that should be continually going on in a fellowship of God's people.

New believers have little knowledge of the Word of God

Those who have been Christians for years often find it difficult to put themselves into the shoes of converts because they do not realise how much their thinking has become moulded by the Word of God. They take their knowledge of the Bible largely for granted, and do not appreciate the changes that have taken place in them. Most people today have only a little knowledge of the Bible and there are converts who have some understanding of the fundamentals of the gospel but very little else. It is going to take years of systematic reading of the Bible and teaching through the church's ministry before they have anything like an adequate grasp of Bible truth. We simply have to reckon with this.

Churches are under the authority of the Word of Christ. He walks among the churches and speaks to them by his Spirit through the Word (Revelation 1:12,13; 2:1,7 etc.). The worship, witness and building up of a church must all take place in accordance with the Word of God and through the opening up of the instructions, principles, and examples which the Word contains. Too many churches do not take seriously enough the fact that the Word of Christ is to dwell richly within them (Colossians 3:16). Indeed all the life and activity of the church is to arise out of the indwelling presence of the Word and so new believers will be at a disadvantage. They may well propose or suggest courses of action which might seem quite sensible from a worldly perspective, and it will need wisdom and tact to explain why these cannot be followed. Tension and resentment can easily creep in and so steps need to be taken to prevent them.

New believers can often be enthusiastic and over-eager

New believers often come like a breath of fresh air into a fellowship. Their faith and knowledge of Christ are new and wonderful to them. They are in the joy of their first love. Their enthusiasm for the things of the Lord gives a great impetus to the whole life and work of the church. All this is great gain. But along with these things there may be a lack of judgment. There may be zeal, but not knowledge. There may be a desire to witness which is not matched by understanding or tact, or a desire to get involved in avenues of service which are not wise. Along with this there can be an impatience with older Christians who try to urge caution upon them. The potential for discord in this is very great, and there are churches who have lost recent believers because they have not known how to handle such a situation.

At the same time many Christians look back on their early days as believers and wish they had been wiser in the way in which they had witnessed. Some feel they spoke unwisely to unbelieving marriage partners. Some regret the confrontational and almost impertinent way in which they spoke to their parents about Christ. Others feel they have lost opportunities to help others because of their brashness as young believers. They may be too hard on themselves in this respect, but these experiences confirm the need for guiding the enthusiasm of those in the first flush of their love for Christ.

New believers can sometimes be greatly disillusioned by older Christians and by churches

Some older Christians, unfortunately, can act like a wet blanket dampening all the enthusiasm of recent converts and younger believers. Sometimes, too, immature believers can be greatly stumbled by the carnal attitudes or actual sins of those who they supposed to be godly men or women, though those with more experience, and with a deeper knowledge of their own hearts and the power of temptation are not affected to the same extent. A knowledge of Scripture and its blunt record of the dreadful falls of men like David and Peter, and the apostasy of people like Saul, Judas and Demas, preserves us from the disillusionment which might otherwise arise.

Some believers can be shocked and distressed by their first experience of a church meeting. In independent churches such meetings have a very important role in the direction of the affairs of the church. Unfortunately they are sometimes occasions when prejudice and entrenched positions are much more in evidence than a submission to the Word of God and a prayerful desire to come to a common understanding of the church's path ahead. Such meetings make real demands upon the members in terms of love, humility, unity, spirituality and prayerfulness. They must never be thought of in terms of democracy with everyone having the right to his or her own opinion and the opportunity to express it, but rather in terms of the body of believers having the mind of Christ (1 Corinthians 2:16; cf. 6:1-5), and for that to be expressed as the church depends upon the Holy Spirit and searches the Scriptures together.

However, while it is right to understand that younger and immature believers can be a source of discord within a church, there is no inevitability about this. We must be aware of potential problems, but new believers often bring a freshness and zeal which helps to promote growth and unity. There is nothing like a number of conversions to stir up a church and to give it a new sense of purpose.

LONGSTANDING MEMBERS AND THE PERILS OF FAMILIARITY

Discord can also often arise from those who have been believers for a long time, and especially when they have spent most of their Christian lives in the same church. Let us consider some of the perils and problems in this case.

Older believers often get set in their ways
This is not wholly bad. We live in days when there is little stability and a great deal of change. Some Christians seem to be unsettled and unsure, changing their mind and altering their ways throughout their Christian lives. This is thoroughly undesirable. A heart which is fixed on God and a mind which is settled in the truth are fundamental for godliness and growth, and for spiritual stability. 'Stand firm. Let nothing move you. Always give yourselves fully to the work of the Lord...' is a vital exhortation for today (1 Corinthians 15:58).

However there are various sorts of immovability! There is the immovability of the tree which has deep roots and which flourishes and produces flowers and fruit, and there is the immovability of a post which is stuck in concrete! Believers who are set in their ways can often be a source of discord, particularly if these are simply based on tradition, or are ways into which they have slipped over the years, and have no desire to change. As we get older we tend to prefer what we are familiar with. Jesus understood this when he said, 'And no one after drinking old wine, wants the new; for he says, "The old is better"'(Luke 5:39). All sorts of arguments and reasons expressed within churches about possible alterations come down to this, 'The old is better!' The old is not better because it is old, nor is the new better because it is new.

A great deal of the rigidity of longstanding members comes down to self-centredness, 'I have come to my conclusions and I am not going to move!' 'Sheer cussedness' may be a rather down-to-earth description, but the thing itself is far more ugly than the word. It is easy enough to impute all sorts of motives to others; it is easy to dismiss all proposals for doing things differently as evidence of ignorance, unspirituality or a love of novelty, but if we are going to be honest we must be prepared to examine our own hearts and motives. There are times when it is right to dig one's heels in; there are causes which are important enough for that. Equally there are times when alteration is demanded by biblical considerations or by new circumstances, and when it can become sinful to resist change. And there are other times when principle is not at stake and when flexibility is a sign of magnanimity and evidence of grace and wisdom.

Older believers can become complacent

Complacency is a very dangerous spiritual disease, and in the nature of the case it is older believers who are prone to it. It was the sin of the church at Laodicea (Revelation 3:14-22), 'I am rich; I have acquired wealth and do not need a thing...' This sort of self-satisfaction is actually more likely to be felt by Christians in a church where there has been a measure of the blessing of the Lord and where there is a relative stability and a sense of God's presence. Perhaps complacency is one of the reasons why churches which have grown and become strong and vigorous begin to decline and break out into all sorts of discord and squabbling.

As in the case of Laodicea such a state of affairs can only come about when people are ignorant of their true condition. Those believers who walk humbly with God and who examine themselves and their attitudes in the light of the word of God will be preserved. Tragically it is possible for Christians to feel that as they get more established in the faith so there is less need to watch and pray and less need for using before God the words of Psalm 139:23,24, 'Search me, O God, and know my heart; test me, and know my anxious thoughts. See if there is any offensive way in me, and lead me in the way everlasting.' The Bible has too many examples of those who began well but who did not end well for any of us to slack off as we grow older in the life of faith (consider for, example, Solomon or the old prophet of 1 Kings 13).

Complacency can sometimes affect a whole church. In these circumstances anyone who tries to awaken the church to its real condition will be looked upon as a disturber of the peace. But in reality such disturbance is to be earnestly desired. Complacent tranquillity is not the harmony that the New Testament urges upon us. Elijah was looked upon as the troubler of Israel by Ahab, but he was actually the voice of the living God to recall a nation to its true allegiance (1 Kings 18:17ff.).

Older believers may grow over-familiar with holy things

Becoming over-familiar with holy things is a very subtle danger, and one that is ever-present. There are some believers whose very service for the Lord exposes them to the danger of losing a sense of holy reverence and fear in dealing with the things of the Lord. I am thinking here of people like stewards, organists or those who are responsible for recording the services. On occasions some of these may be in a service of worship, but not of it! For example, someone video-recording a worship service may be utterly unmoved by all that is happening; he can be detached, a spectator. If people can become detached and uninvolved spiritually in services of worship, how much more likely is it that they will approach the whole of the Lord's work in that sort of way?

The person who is exposed to this more than any other is the pastor and some churches have suffered terribly as a result. The pastor or minister of the Word gets acquainted with leading services; with praying, with handling and preaching the Word of God, with conducting the Lord's Supper. Somehow it becomes almost automatic to him to do these things. He learns to be able to do them when he has had very little time to prepare; when he is very tired; when quite frankly he would rather not do them. Imperceptibly if he is not careful he can minister the means of grace without depending on grace himself and without them being a means of grace to him. And this spills over into all his work. It is a recipe for trouble and discord. Familiarity with holy things without a sense of their reality, must be guarded against like the plague.

This does not always lead to discord, sometimes it leads to a general deadness and sense of the unreality of spiritual things settling over the congregation. More usually, however, people who have become insensitive in this way become proud, prickly, self-opinionated; just the characteristics which provoke discord.

Older believers easily forget past struggles

It is amazing how forgetful we can be. Most Christians develop in their Christian lives over the years, experiencing many difficulties, not a few falls and periods of backsliding. Only gradually did most of us come to understand truths which now seem patently obvious to us whenever we open our Bibles. How much most of us owe to the patience and wisdom of Christian friends, usually older, who bore with our immaturity and weaknesses and helped us through times of temptation and testing. How much we relied on the advice and guidance of pastors and elders in our early days of witness and service for Christ. Yet the extraordinary thing is that we can forget all this so easily.

So instead of being sympathetic to younger believers in their struggles, and a source of wise advice and support, older Christians can sometimes be just the opposite. This is very sad in at least two ways. First of all because the experience which the older believer has gained over years is being forgotten and wasted, instead of being used in the service of the Lord and for the good of the church. But secondly because of the discouragement which it is to younger believers themselves and the discord which it provokes. A little honest looking back would be of great value to not a few older believers.

Older believers may be impatient with younger people

Some longstanding members of churches seem to imagine that no believer ought really to propose any course of action until they have been in the church for twenty years or more. They develop a possessive attitude to the church. It is 'their' church; they have supported the work for years; they have given to it; they have worked hard. All this may be true, for it is sometimes those who have been very faithful over many years who later on develop this sort of attitude.

Such an attitude tends to look with suspicion at all recent additions to the church and especially young people—unless they confirm all the ideas and opinions of the older members. It views younger people as 'upstarts', that is people who have no real right to be voicing any opinion or making any suggestion. That there are young people who sometimes speak very foolishly and who are out of place is undoubted, but the same can be true of older people too. As people begin to get on in years they find it difficult to admit new ideas into their thinking, and they seem to get more impatient—this often happens whether people are Christians or not. The same crustiness can be found in older believers as is found in unbelievers.

This is inevitably a source of tension and often discord in a fellowship. Perhaps the key to preventing it lies earlier on in the life of the believer in a self-awareness that such attitudes must be guarded against and positive alternatives must be so rooted in the life and outlook that they do not wither with age. What we are considering here is little short of a tragedy because quite apart from the harm it does to the fellowship as a whole and perhaps to younger believers, it often means that Christians spend their last days rather embittered and distressed. Not a few older Christians find themselves out of sympathy with what is happening in the church to which they have given years of support and service. They do not want to leave and often there is no satisfactory alternative church to go to in any case. At this point we are considering the fact that older people can sometimes bring such distressing circumstances upon themselves, though we must add that often it is thoughtless, insensitive and sometimes unbiblical changes brought in by another generation which are responsible.

It is also true that large numbers of longstanding members have proved by the grace of God to be the backbone of the churches. Those who, in the providence of God, are able to stay for many years in the same church exercising a godly influence and setting an example for all to follow, are a great asset. When those of wisdom and experience, settled in the faith, work harmoniously together with those who are younger and full of enthusiasm and energy there is potential for real growth and for much glory to be brought to God.

QUESTIONS FOR STUDY AND DISCUSSION

1. How can Christians get to know their own weaknesses?

2. What steps can be taken to help integrate new members into a church?

3. What are the dangers of spiritual 'middle-age'?

4. In what ways should longstanding Christians exert their influence in a church?

5. Case study: How does James 3:13-18 help us in promoting good relationships in a church?

From within the Church

I n exploring the reasons for discord in the church we still keep our eye on internal factors. There are many things that can go wrong. It is possible to misunderstand the sort of harmony that is to be pursued. It is possible for leaders to misunderstand their role, or go about fulfilling it in mistaken or inadequate ways. What the Lord has provided to promote the health of the church can sometimes have the opposite effect.

MISUNDERSTANDINGS ABOUT HARMONY

Harmony does not mean complete agreement about everything
Some people think that harmony in the church means everyone agreeing on every point, but this rarely happens. It is quite unrealistic to expect nearly complete agreement, and idealistic and unrealisable expectations are a particularly potent source of discord. All Christians are agreed about certain things, but because of their background and upbringing, because of their different levels of understanding, the fact that some have been taught for years from Scripture while others haven't, and the different ideas they accepted while unconverted, there is going to be a wide variety of views on some topics.

It is quite clear that there was considerable diversity of understanding and viewpoint amongst the Christians in the New Testament churches. Those from a Jewish background saw things differently from those from a Gentile background. In fact the early churches were commanded to make concessions to Jewish sensitivities. This was partly for evangelistic purposes, but it was also to reduce tension among believers (Acts 15; see also 21:25). Not surprisingly this whole matter of differing viewpoints had to be tackled in some of Paul's letters. In 1 Corinthians he goes into some detail about the differing attitudes among the believers to eating meat which had been offered to idols. This was a source of division within the church, and Paul was much more concerned to ensure that the Christians had a right attitude to each other than to tell them exactly what to do. His approach to the Roman believers is the same: Romans 14, where the problems were similar though not identical. He sets out a number of principles which are still essential for promoting harmony in a church.

Those who are stronger in the faith and understanding (or who think they are!), are not to despise those who feel they ought only to eat vegetables, because they look upon meat as unclean (v.3). He is unsparing in his words, 'You, then, why do you judge your brother? Or why do you look down on your brother?' (v.10). On matters like this everyone is to be convinced in his own mind (v.5). There may be discussion between believers, but each has his own conscience before the Lord and has to come to his own understanding, and must not be browbeaten or ridiculed into changing his mind.

So Paul says in v.13 'Therefore let us stop passing judgment on one another. Instead, make up your mind not to put any stumbling-block or obstacle in your brother's way.' A further principle is this, 'Let us therefore make every effort to do what leads to peace and to mutual edification' (v.19). Another principle shows that part of the problem was that some were getting things quite out of proportion and this had to be corrected, 'For the kingdom of God is not a matter of eating and drinking, but of righteousness, peace and joy in the Holy Spirit' (v.17).

Paul's argument here is often misunderstood and misapplied. It is often said that what Paul is speaking about are things which are 'indifferent', things which were really very small and unimportant. By comparison the things about which we disagree, it is argued, are much more vital and therefore what Paul says here cannot be applied to them. These 'indifferent' matters, however, were not small or unimportant at all to those who were concerned about them. As far as they were concerned to eat meat defiled them in the sight of God; it meant disobedience to God and left them unclean before him. So also with the observance of days (vv.5,6). It was not a matter of indifference to those who believed they were under divine obligation to keep them. Their conscience before God was involved. In his discussion Paul is primarily speaking to those who realised it was not necessary to abstain from meat or to observe special days. The point which he makes to them is that as the kingdom of heaven is not primarily about such things but is about righteousness, peace and joy, they can safely leave off arguing and trying to compel their fellow Christians to follow their practice, and rather promote these gracious qualities which will be a real blessing in the church whatever attitude is taken to these other matters. There is also the implication that those with more sensitive consciences ought not to try and impose their views and practices upon their brothers or sisters. Nowadays they would probably set up their own churches so that they would all be able to worship according to conscience, as they understood it!

We are still very slow to learn the lessons that these chapters teach. We are not to spend our time trying to get agreement on all the minutiae of doctrine or of practice. We may need to discuss some of them but an atmosphere of righteousness, peace and joy brought about by the Holy Spirit is the best atmosphere for that, and one in which greater degrees of agreement are likely to be reached. And where agreement isn't reached at least there will be mutual respect, a clearer understanding of each other, and a gracious forebearance of differing viewpoints—harmony in fact!

Agreement in doctrine?
Most Christians recognise that in the realm of Christian practice and behaviour we have to allow for some diversity within the church. Doctrine seems another matter, but it cannot really be, because the same Scripture that lays the foundation of teaching also regulates our conduct. So is doctrinal diversity permissible; and if it is what are its limits?

These questions are extremely difficult, and saying that different answers are bound to be given only highlights the problem! Some churches make a clear distinction between what are called fundamental doctrines and others which do not lie so close to the centre of saving truth. That there is such a distinction can scarcely be doubted and in some respects most Christians and churches operate with it—perhaps in inter-church relationships for example. When it comes to drawing a clear line between fundamental and non-fundamental truths it becomes much more difficult. After all what we really want is a biblical differentiation between the two, but that is not so easy to find. Some important principles can be stated.

First, there are certainly a number of biblical truths which are funda-mental for an understanding of salvation and these should be clearly affirmed and taught by churches. We live in days when clear doctrinal preaching is very much out of favour, and it is time to redress the balance in this respect.

Conversely churches cannot allow those who teach the opposite of these truths to remain within their ranks. There is such a thing as heresy, however unpopular it may be to say so today. To deny vital truth revealed in the Bible is not to dissent from another's viewpoint, it is to pit oneself against God.

Further we need to draw a distinction between those who oppose biblical teaching and those who have limited understanding, or who come from backgrounds where they have learnt very little biblical truth. Those who deny basic truths; who try to undermine them by bringing in other doctrines, or who simply reject them, have to be dealt with very firmly and unless they show signs of repentance should have no place within a church. Those who are simply confused and in a real muddle are in a very different position, though it may be a difficult and time-consuming thing to set them right.

Many errors have very serious spiritual consequences in the lives of Christians and within the churches. Prosperity teaching or false views of prophecy have done immense damage both in individual lives and to churches. The New Testament never treats heresy as simply an academic matter. Peter, for example, warns of false teachers who 'will secretly introduce destructive heresies' (2 Peter 2:1).

It is good to have strong convictions, but if a person has the same strength of conviction about every point of doctrine there is probably something wrong. If we are intended to grow in grace and a knowledge of Jesus Christ then it presupposes that our knowledge of Jesus Christ is limited to begin with. Such a knowledge involves doctrinal under-standing and grows by increasing understanding of the Scriptures. It is the experience of most believers that though their fundamental beliefs may not change over the years, yet their understanding of the balance and proportion of truth and the relationships between truths does grow and change.

Some Christians seem to think not only that all truths are on the same level, but that they are all linked indissolubly together. So they are not able to contemplate altering at one point without the whole fabric of their Christian faith seeming threatened. This prevents people from even considering alternative understandings of Scripture which other believers may hold, and is bound to lead to tension within a church.

Finally, if believers emphasise some point of doctrine in a way which leads to a faction being formed in the church that can very easily lead to party-spirit and divisiveness. To have groups trying to promote a particular view of sanctification, or of the Lord's return, to mention two possibilities, easily leads to dissension. There is a very fine balance here. If diversity is allowable, factiousness is not.

There is bound to be some doctrinal diversity within churches. A basic statement of faith that defines the fundamentals may not always seem adequate. On the other hand a much more detailed statement requires a certain latitude of interpretation. For example, whether God is capable of suffering is surely something about which different interpretations are allowable. What is especially needful in these days are leaders who 'can encourage others by sound doctrine and refute those who oppose it' (Titus 1:9).

Agreeing to disagree

The expression 'agreeing to disagree' has its dangers, especially as it does not put any limits on disagreement, nor does it indicate that through the Word of God believers should gradually be brought to a greater agreement amongst themselves. Nevertheless it says what will be needed for harmony in a church.

A church is not to be thought of as a sort of religious club. Clubs usually have a series of aims and rules which everyone who belongs to them agrees with when they join; usually they join because they already agree and wish to be involved in the activity of the club and promote its aims. A church may seem to be a very similar organism, and some churches have basic documents of beliefs, aims and conduct which give that impression.

However, a church is not a club set up by people, it is a divine institution. It is a fellowship of those who have been born again by the Holy Spirit and who thus believe in Jesus Christ. It is much more like a family. When believers are first brought into the church it is like when children are born into a family. Just as babies disrupt the neat order of family life established before their birth, so the coming of new believers may well disrupt the life of the church. Babies come in a variety of shapes and sizes; some are good, but others are very demanding. As they grow they have their questions and problems; they bring joy and can contribute greatly to the life of the family; they may bring heartache and sorrow, all the more so because they are family members.

If a church is run like a club it can avoid quite a lot of the problems of family life; but if it is recognised as being a local family of the people of God then it has to prepare itself for the demands that that will make on all the membership and the leaders. In many nonconformist churches believers are baptized and enter membership on a credible profession of faith and after some basic instruction. This seems wise and there are biblical grounds for such an approach, but a profession of faith is made credible primarily by evidences of spiritual life. It is possible, however, to make entrance into a church a far more demanding thing than it is in the New Testament. This may ensure a greater unity in the church, and do away with problems of growth, but the result is that new converts may be kept out of membership when they ought to be in, or they may go elsewhere, or perhaps the Lord may not grant many to such churches.

There is also the question of believers from other areas and other churches joining the church. In New Testament days when believers moved they naturally joined the church in the place to which they moved. Ideally that should be the same today, but in the present situation it is not as simple as that. Care should be taken so that churches do not have constitutions which are so detailed that only a very limited number of believers can come into membership. In such circumstances Christians may regularly attend but never actually come into membership. This easily leads to tensions. Once such people get established they naturally develop friendships within the church. As a result they may have quite considerable influence. However they are not officially subject to the leadership, they do not have to agree to any of the decisions of the church meeting, and it is not possible to discipline them effectively should that be necessary. None of this is very satisfactory. If they are simply being prevented from membership because the church has a constitution which they cannot honestly agree with, then it may be right for this to be reconsidered to see if it is more detailed than it needs to be. In the case of a trust deed this is not possible for trust deeds are legal documents which must be honoured by churches. Care should be taken in drawing them up to avoid binding future generations unnecessarily.

Churches should not restrict themselves to very narrow and limited view-points. It is perfectly possible for a group of people all to harp on the same string: that produces a melody, but not harmony. There is a basic unity which is fundamental, 'There is one body and one Spirit—just as you were called to one hope when you were called—one Lord, one faith, one baptism; one God and Father of all, who is over all and through all and in all.' But there is a corporate unity which we have yet to arrive at, 'until we all reach unity in the faith and in the knowledge of the Son of God and become mature, attaining to the whole measure of the fulness of Christ' (Ephesians 4:4-6,13).

Leadership

However there cannot be the same latitude of understanding among leaders as among the rest of the membership. At a purely practical level that is simply inviting trouble. The leaders in the New Testament were men of faith, spirituality and doctrinal grasp. The first leaders were the apostles. They had spent three years with Jesus himself. Even after the resurrection the Lord continued to speak to them 'about the kingdom of God' (Acts 1:3). The early believers 'devoted themselves to the apostles' teaching', teaching which the apostles were all agreed about and which they patiently taught to the church. Paul was very concerned about the 'succession' of apostolic teaching being continued in the churches and so in 2 Timothy 2:2 he says, 'And the things you have heard me say in the presence of many witnesses entrust to reliable men who will also be qualified to teach others.' It is essential that leaders have a good grasp of biblical teaching themselves as well as the ability to pass this on to others.

Leaders sometimes change their doctrinal position while in office and this has harmed many churches. For one reason or another they do a *volte-face* on a point of doctrine, and in the first flush of coming to accept something new they are usually very keen to bring everyone else to their new understanding. There is no quick solution to this problem. Some things can be said, however.

It is certainly not living openly as a Christian ought for someone to accept a position of leadership while suppressing the fact that he holds very strongly to a particular point of view. This is particularly repre-hensible if he knows that this viewpoint is not one shared in the church.

If a leader does come to a different understanding of some truth, he ought to make this known openly to his fellow leaders. If relationships are as they should be within the leadership they will probably already be aware of the way he has been thinking and will have discussed the matter with him. In some circumstances a leader must be prepared to resign, or at least offer his resignation, in the interests of the welfare of the whole body. Usually he will know whether his new viewpoint is likely to cause difficulties within the leadership and in the church.

If he does resign he must still be very careful and put the interests of the church first. He must not think he can now speak out on the back benches, and begin to form a faction or agitate for change. The matter is a delicate one because a situation which allows for no alteration at all cannot be right. Just as individuals need to be searching the Scriptures ready to receive new light from them, so churches don't have everything right and there must always be room for reformation and accepting new insights from the Word of God. Generally speaking, though, we should expect a leadership to come to new understandings of Scripture together. Where leaders are simply blinkered or where individuals jump to new conclusions, tensions and problems are likely to develop and all leaders should be sensitively aware of the difficulties at this point.

LACK OF PASTORAL CARE

By leaders

The New Testament clearly expects that within each church there will be those set apart for teaching the Word of God and pastoral care. Spiritual oversight, shepherdly care for the people of God, is a vital necessity. These references make this clear, Acts 20:28; 1 Timothy 3:1-5; Hebrews 13:17; 1 Peter 5:1-4. A lack of wise and sensitive shepherding of the flock is almost an open invitation for tensions and dispute.

Some churches fail to set aside anyone for this vital task. One of the first things Paul and Barnabas did on their missionary journeys after a church was formed was to ensure that it had an oversight of elders, Acts 14:23. Paul's instruction to Titus also shows that without elders a church is lacking something essential (Titus 1:5). In the case of small churches who do not have anyone suitable for oversight the best answer may be to seek for a measure of pastoral oversight from within a larger church. Sometimes churches do not have oversight because they do not feel able to support a pastor; sometimes because they are wedded to a view of democracy which comes from human society rather than the Word of God. At other times the problem is that those with responsibilities to oversee the church are either not fitted for the work, or at any rate do not fulfil their responsibilities. Churches must realise their need of pastoral care and oversight; those appointed to carry out these functions must be responsible and diligent in carrying them out.

One reason why pastoral care is sometimes inadequate is that pastors give themselves so much to the ministry of the Word that they do not have time to watch out for pastoral needs or to visit and talk with members regularly. One of the benefits of having other elders working in co-operation is that the pastor can give himself more particularly to the Word and prayer. A great deal of pastoral care should take place through the ministry of the Word, and for this to be done adequately the preaching needs to be applicatory and to address the actual needs of the members and their situations.

By the members themselves

Many verses of Scripture indicate that members of a church should care for each other and encourage each other; see, for example, Philippians 2:3-11; 1 Thessalonians 5:11,14,15; and Hebrews 10:24,25. It is very easy for this to get overlooked. Some members think that because the minister and any other elders are responsible for pastoral care they have no need to do anything themselves. Conversely some in oversight give the impression that they don't want anyone else interfering with it. However Christian love is bound to express itself practically in loving care and mutual help among members. This is what makes fellowship the distinctive Christian quality that it is. Members will naturally have their own friends and people that they associate with from within the church, often among those of the same age-group or sex. Provided such friendships do not become too exclusive they are a good thing and can be a means by which Christians help, pray for, and support each other. In fact the appointed oversight needs this mutual care to be effective, because it means that wise counsel and help given to one will soon be spread to others as well.

Failure to prepare for difficulties

Part of the responsibility of leaders is to explain to those under their care the nature of the Christian life and the difficulties and spiritual dangers which they are likely to face. In the early days the churches faced outright persecution and Paul prepared his converts for this and did his best to encourage and help them when it came. In Acts 14:22 we read of Paul and Barnabas returning to the cities where they had made converts, 'strengthening the disciples and encouraging them to remain true to the faith. "We must go through many hardships to enter the kingdom of God," they said. Similarly Paul writes to the Thessalonians like this; 'We sent Timothy, who is our brother and God's fellow-worker in spreading the gospel of Christ, to strengthen and encourage you in your faith, so that no-one would be unsettled by these trials. You know quite well that we were destined for them. In fact, when we were with you, we kept telling you that we would be persecuted. And it turned out that way, as you well know' (1 Thessalonians 3:2-4). The wisdom of Paul is plain to see in these references. Similarly Christians should be prepared for all the various temptations and problems of the life of faith so that no one will be unsettled when they come. Church life is not always easy. Paul had to warn the elders of the Ephesian church that there would be severe problems arising from within the church just as there would be attacks from outside (Acts 20:29,30). Wise pastoral care helps people to foresee and be prepared for the difficulties and discipline of church relationships.

Failure to spot early signs of trouble

Hebrews 13:17 tells us that leaders are to 'keep watch over' those under their care, 'as men who must give an account'. If this is faithfully carried out then tensions and relationship difficulties will be spotted early on and can be tackled before relationships have become really strained and people have begun to take up entrenched positions. If the work of watching over souls is not carried out as it ought to be then a situation may easily get out of hand.

Look at how Jesus Christ anticipated Peter's fall and both warned him beforehand and prayed for him and the other disciples (Luke 22:31-34). We do not have the knowledge that he did, but we can anticipate how the devil may try and exploit situations to his own advantage, as Paul says, 'We are not unaware of his schemes' (2 Corinthians 2:11). We do not know the hearts of others but if we hear Christians speaking over self-confidently as Peter did then we can expect a fall, and both warn, pray and prepare for what might happen.

Another interesting passage is Acts 21:20-26. Paul has come to Jerusalem and is told how many of the believing Jews, who are still zealous for the law, have been informed that he teaches Jews to forsake Moses by saying they ought not to circumcise their children nor keep the Jewish customs. He is advised to join four men who had a vow in order to prevent criticism and avoid a potentially very damaging dispute and possible division within the church at Jerusalem. So Paul took the men and went to the temple with them. That led directly to his arrest after unbelieving Jews stirred up the people against him. He took the action he did in order to try and maintain harmony within the church. It led to danger and imprisonment for him, but it seems to have served its purpose as far as the church was concerned. Wise pastoral care will try to prevent potential trouble arising either by anticipating it or trying to catch it early on.

HEAVY-HANDED PASTORAL CARE

Interference

If too little pastoral care can lead to trouble so also can pastoral care which becomes obsessive and possessive. Perhaps as a reaction against the slackness of care perceived to be the case in a number of churches in recent times, a pastoral care has developed that goes beyond what the Scripture indicates and interferes in personal and family life. Some reports of this may well be exaggerated but they point up a danger which does exist and which can certainly lead to discord. The Lord has not given leaders the power to pry into every corner of the lives of church members. It is worth bearing in mind what Paul, an apostle after all, wrote, 'Not that we lord it over your faith, but we work with you for your joy' (2 Corinthians 1:24).

The way in which Paul describes himself is also significant. He writes as a father on some occasions (1 Corinthians 4:15), while on another he describes himself as a mother to the believers, 'But we were gentle among you, like a mother caring for her little children. We loved you so much that we were delighted to share with you not only the gospel of God, but our lives as well, because you had become so dear to us' (1 Thessalonians 2:7,8). The description sometimes used of what we are warning against, 'heavy shepherding', is really a contradiction in terms.

Regimentation

Another danger is that of over-organising the church to such an extent that regimentation takes place. We find martial language in the New Testament and the Christian is pictured as a soldier. Nowhere however is the church pictured as an army and even less is there any suggestion that church leaders are to be thought of as officers. This is not intended as a reflection on the Salvation Army; it is a warning against authoritarianism in the church, against leaders with a sergeant major mentality, and a situation in which members have their lives and their time subjected to a military-style discipline. This is the way of some of the cults and in the end it is bound to lead to division and hurt.

Exhortation, strong appeals from the Word of God, and encouragement are perfectly proper, but balance and proportion, which are admittedly difficult in many situations, have to be preserved. There has to be organisation in a church if it is going to function efficiently. There has to be a sharing out of responsibilities; there have to be rotas and commitment to fulfilling certain tasks on the part of members. At the same time this must not be rigid and burdensome. Members are to understand that their obligations are to Christ. They should serve out of love for him.

It is true that God uses people with strong personalities and the ability to motivate others. Yet such gifts must not be abused. Fear or guilt should never be used to coerce people into doing the Lord's work. The personalities of members should be respected. God has not made us all alike and does not intend us all to serve in exactly the same way. In an army individuality has to be knocked out of recruits; then they have to be knocked into shape, know how to fall into line and march together. However in a church, discipline and order come much more from the example of leaders and from the love of Christ impelling self-discipline and co-operation.

Christian freedom

The world has seen many authoritarian regimes, workers have suffered under heavy-handed employers, and the same has often been true in the sphere of religion. The teachers of the law and Pharisees of Christ's day were guilty of this; 'They tie up heavy loads, and put them on men's shoulders,' said Jesus (Matthew 23:4). It was against this background that he spoke some of his most well-known words, 'Come to me, all you who are weary and burdened, and I will give you rest. Take my yoke upon you and learn from me, for I am gentle and humble in heart, and you will find rest for your souls. For my yoke is easy and my burden is light" (Matthew 11:28-30). The contrast is vivid: against the authoritarian religion of the scribes and Pharisees who laid heavy burdens upon people arising from human traditions which had developed over the years, Christ promised rest, an easy yoke and a light burden. Christianity is first and foremost a relationship with Jesus Christ, one who, unlike many others, is gentle and humble in heart, who never throws his weight about, whose understanding and compassion are perfect, who does not break bruised reeds nor quench smoking flax (Matthew 12:20).

Christ sets people free. Free from condemnation and sin, but also free from bondage to other people and their opinions, traditions and commandments. Sadly, however, even in the early churches this freedom was often threatened. To the Colossians Paul wrote, 'Since you died with Christ to the basic principles of the world, why, as though you still belonged to it, do you submit to its rules; "Do not handle! Do not taste! Do not touch!"? These are all destined to perish with use, because they are based on human commands and teachings.' (2:20-22). He seems even more concerned in his letter to the Galatians, 'But now that you know God—or rather are known by God—how is it that you are turning back to those weak and miserable principles? Do you want to be enslaved by them all over again? You are observing special days and months and seasons and years. I fear for you, that somehow I have wasted my efforts for you' (4:9-11). And again, 'It is for freedom that Christ has set us free. Stand firm, then, and do not be burdened again by a yoke of slavery'(5:1).

This is a theme which is not often dwelt on, nor understood, in these days. Christian service is not like service in other areas of life. Working together in a church proceeds on quite different principles to those which obtain in secular organisations. Leadership is exercised in quite different ways in churches from the way it usually operates in society. Everything centres around and springs from Jesus Christ, and the freedom and rest we experience in him. Tensions will arise and relationships be strained unless all the members of the church are first of all living in a genuine relationship with him. When things go wrong the first essential is a return to Christ. Nothing can be right until things are right with him.

Learning from Christ

At the heart of the words of Jesus Christ we have been considering, comes the phrase 'take my yoke upon you and learn from me'. The Christian life is one of growth and learning, but it is not just a matter of the mind being informed with correct teaching and then living by what has been learnt. The twelve disciples learnt from Christ in experience as they had taken up his yoke and went with him, and served with him. Theirs was the learning of apprenticeship. Similarly, though now in a spiritual way, Christians learn from Jesus Christ today. Yoked to him, and so strengthened by him, in daily life, in the fellowship of the church, we learn from him. This personal element in Christian learning and discipleship is vital. It is in-service learning; learning in life from Jesus Christ. Churches need to understand this. For example, sermons and teaching in the church are occasions when the word of Christ and the presence of Christ should be experienced together. It is the voice of Christ, by means of the written Word and through the Holy Spirit, that is to be heard. This is of fundamental importance. Only Christ has the authority to command his disciples; only Christ is adequate to comfort them. As Paul says in Colossians 3:16, 'Let the word of Christ dwell in you richly'.

There is a further aspect of this which needs to be noted. The disciples of Christ were often very slow to learn. Their reactions and responses were sometimes very far from what they ought to have been to the words of their Lord. But with patience and wisdom the Lord went on teaching them. They did not grasp everything all at once. Even after three years there were still things which they could not yet bear (John 16:12). The disciples went through a learning process in which even their faults and mistakes were used by Christ (see eg. Luke 22:31,32). It is still the same. We do not learn everything all at once. Just as Christ bore with his disciples we have to bear with one another. Just as he was kind, wise and patient, so we have to develop the same qualities and show them to each other. The important thing is that we are learning from him.

FAILURE TO DISCIPLINE

Restoring a brother

In Matthew 18:15-21 Jesus explains to his disciples how a brother who has sinned is to be restored. Here he is dealing directly with a relationship between two believers which has been broken by the sin of one of them. If relationships are to be restored and maintained within the church these words of Christ must be obeyed. The purpose is to restore relationships: 'if he listens to you, you have won your brother over' (v.15). The onus is put upon the one who has been wronged. If he has been sinned against and hurt, then he is to go and see the offending brother, or sister, privately and see if the matter can be cleared up there and then.

This is of course not always easy. It is much easier to talk to some sympathetic friend, who will then pass it round the whole church, than to speak directly to the person concerned. It is easy to argue that he ought to come and apologise to you. It is true he should, and if he does there is no problem, but if he doesn't then the words of the Lord apply, 'Go and show him his fault just between the two of you'. It is probable that disobedience to these instructions of Christ are responsible for most of the relationship problems within churches. A true, loving desire to put relationships right and a willingness to obey the Lord's instructions would surely prevent many situations which develop and fester, poisoning the atmosphere among Christians sometimes over a period of years.

Dealing with the problem

Our Lord recognises that speaking to a brother or sister privately will not always be enough. Experience shows that this is so. Sometimes the offending brother will not listen at all; sometimes he rejects the charge that has been made, sometimes he blames the person who has come to him. So Christ has set out a pattern which is to be followed; first two or three more; if he will not hear them, then take it to the whole church; if he will not listen to the church, then he is to be treated as an unbeliever.

At this point it is not the pattern itself which we want to consider, rather what the effect of using it will entail. Right from the beginning the problem is being dealt with. So often disputes and broken relationships are left until both sides have taken up entrenched positions, the original problem has almost been lost sight of, and everything only comes out into the open when it seems almost impossible to know what the facts are or to put things right. Even if the initial going to the brother who has sinned bears no fruit, from then on the situation does not just depend on the two persons concerned. Others have been brought in to help and a process begun which has one of two clear ends in view. It is no longer just a personal matter, if necessary it becomes a church matter. This is a great help and limits the possible damage.

Repentance and forgiveness

The object in going to the one who has sinned is to secure repentance, and the one who goes must be prepared to forgive. It was doubtless the implications of this preparedness to forgive which led Peter to the question he asked in v.21, 'Lord, how many times shall I forgive my brother when he sins against me? Up to seven times?'

It can scarcely be stressed enough that repentance is an element in the Christian life which every believer should often express. As often as we sin, so often should we repent. It is comparatively easy to express our repentance to God in prayer, especially about general rather than specific sins. Or at least that is what we often feel; when we are truly convicted before the Lord repentance is a bitter experience, even though it leads to the joy of cleansing and restoration. But it certainly is not easy to admit our sins in true repentance before our brothers and sisters, and ask forgiveness for specific sins of word or act. So often our repentance and apology is qualified; so often we make excuses; so often we insinuate that they are really half to blame. True forgiveness and restoration cannot thrive in an atmosphere of half-hearted repentance.

Just as repentance is not easy, so also full-hearted forgiveness is not easy either. It is just as easy to forgive reluctantly, or to qualify our forgiveness or to add in a little reminder for the future just to make sure! If there are going to be right relationships within a church then we have got to start obeying the words of Christ. There has to be loving confrontation after sin. There has to be proper repentance and apology. There has to be loving forgiveness which, if necessary, will be repeated again and again, even 'up to seventy times seven' (Matthew 18:22; NKJV).

Excommunication

If however neither personal conversation, nor discussion with several others, nor the approach of the church results in repentance then the offender has to be treated as 'a pagan or a tax-collector.' This means that the person is being put back into the position of an unbeliever. This must be done because if a member refuses to listen to the church then his continued presence is bound to be a source of tension. To refuse the verdict and appeal that is made to him is a very serious matter. In such cases a church must be concerned for the restoration of the one who has sinned, but if it is not possible to bring this about, to allow the person in the church out of the mistaken hope that he may yet change is simply asking for trouble. Some churches have no mechanism by which they can express a corporate appeal to a member, and this itself is a source of weakness and may lead to discord and failure to deal with problems adequately.

In 1 Corinthians 5 Paul is also explicit about what is to be done when someone has sinned and he cannot be brought to repentance, 'hand this man over to Satan so that the sinful nature may be destroyed and his spirit saved on the day of the Lord' (v.5). The first reason for taking this action is the restoration of the person concerned. But Paul is also concerned for the church as well, 'Don't you know that a little yeast works through the whole batch of dough? Get rid of the old yeast that you may be a new batch without yeast—as you really are.' 'Expel the wicked man from among you' (v.6,7,13). Harmony within the church depends on people who refuse to listen to it, those who have sinned and who will not repent, those who are heretical and factious (Romans 16:17; 2 Thessalonians 3:6,14) being put outside where they cannot harm its unity. Love for the members demands that this be done, as well as the reputation of the church, the glory of Christ, and the best interests of those who are disciplined. We shirk this responsibility placed upon us by Christ at our peril.

BEYOND THE LOCAL CHURCH

Scarcely any church is so neatly packaged that it has no contact with other churches or Christians, but such contact can sometimes be a complicating factor. For example pastoral care and discipline are often undermined because members simply decide to go and worship elsewhere. In some cases those who have been put out of fellowship by one church go and join another, sometimes with no questions asked and no contact made with the first church. This is in no-one's interests. There must be a greater spirit of co-operation and respect for other churches than that.

Another possible source of difficulty arises from what have come to be called para-church organisations. In some cases members have divided loyalties, sometimes it seems as if they have a greater loyalty to the organisation than to the church. This naturally causes tensions. In the main, Christian organisations try to respect the church, but they are not always wise in this. Some organisations seem to try and take over the role of the church in certain respects. In other cases members of particular organisations become pressure groups in their churches. All that is being done at this point is highlighting the possibility of problems so that leaders and members can prayerfully avoid them.

Then there are those who work for Christian organisations but who are members of local churches. These may be highly gifted members. They may seldom be seen in the church because they are out speaking, and perhaps are often away from home. Perhaps the church would like to use their gifts, or some in the church would like them to use their gifts, or they themselves want to use their gifts, in the local church! There has to be realism and honesty among the leaders and such workers. If they belong to the church then they must come under the pastoral care of its leaders. They must remember their example to the rest of the members. As they hope that the church will pray for them, so they should try as often as possible to be in the prayer meeting themselves, taking a lead in prayer. They should only have positions of leadership in the church if they can really fulfil their responsibilities. On the other hand the church should be kept informed about their work, support them and make them feel their work is appreciated and that the church is their spiritual home.

QUESTIONS FOR STUDY AND DISCUSSION

1. In what ways can church members 'spur one another on towards love and good works' (Hebrews 10:24)?

2. What reasons may there be for pastoral care becoming oppressive?

3. When does sin in a Christian become a matter for discipline in the church?

4. Should churches respect each other's discipline; what does this mean in practice?

5. Case study: What limits does 1 Corinthians 8 put on Christian freedom?

From influences outside the Church

Local churches exist in this world. For this reason they, and all their members, are exposed to many influences from outside. It would be a mistake, however, simply to look outside to identify and resist these influences. Their subtlety is the fact that they work within the minds and hearts of believers. Though ultimately from outside, they appear within the churches and powerfully work for discord.

THE WORLD

The world is all-pervasive

In his prayer for his disciples, recorded in John 17, Jesus prayed, 'I have given them your word; and the world has hated them, for they are not of the world, any more than I am of the world. My prayer is not that you take them out of the world but that you protect them from the evil one' (vv.14,15). Here are certain truths about believers and their relationship to the world. They are not of the world, that is they do not belong to it, just as Jesus himself did not. However they remain in it, which is dangerous for them because the world hates them and they are exposed to the evil—and the evil one—which is in the world. The 'world' here is not the physical earth, for 'The earth is the Lord's, and all its fullness.' Nor is it just the world of people considered as those created by God. Rather it is the world of unbelieving people; those whose lives are under the dominion of sin and controlled by the prince of this world.

It is in this world that Christians live and bear their witness. The world is characterised by attitudes which are evil and very harmful. Pride, selfishness, ambition, envy and greed are all attitudes which are typically worldly and which poison so many relationships and cause so much harm in society. Even family life is often spoiled by these things and they bring unhappiness wherever they are found. Because we live in the world, and the influence of the world is around us and on us even when we scarcely realise it, we must be very careful and watch out that worldly attitudes do not creep into our hearts or infiltrate our churches.

The world's ideas appeal to the natural man

'The natural man' is a phrase used by Paul in his first letter to the Corinthians (2:14; NKJV) to refer to people who are not spiritual; that is to those who have not been born again by the Holy Spirit (John 3:5-8). They are ordinary people, fallen because they are descended from Adam, who are unable to appreciate spiritual things; in fact they find them foolish. In the world people think in a 'natural' way; they do not think as Christians think—that is when Christians are thinking as they ought to.

The trouble is that at one time we were all 'natural people'. We were much like everybody else; we thought and acted much as they do. It was natural for us to do so. Of course things became different when we were brought to faith in Jesus Christ. We were given 'the mind of Christ' (1 Corinthians 2:16). We became dissatisfied with our old attitudes and God began to implant new ones within us. However it is still very easy for us to fall into the old way of thinking and feeling. This was the trouble with the Corinthians that Paul was writing to. He also uses another word to describe them, 'carnal'. 'For you are still carnal. For where there are envy, strife, and divisions among you, are you not carnal and behaving like mere men?'(1 Corinthians 3:3; NKJV). These Corinthians were Christians, but they were thinking and acting as they used to do before they were converted. They were behaving like 'mere men'; they were carnal, or fleshly, or, if you like, worldly, in their attitudes. They had not ceased to be Christians, but for the time being at least they were more like the unbelievers they used to be than the Christians they had become. When that happens there will be discord in the church, as the letters to the Corinthians show so clearly.

Part of growing together as members in a church means that we recognise that we all have carnal attitudes which need correcting or removing, and we need to help one another in leaving these things behind and following the will of God together. Where this is not recognised, or where believers are not willing to listen to each other or help each other, then ingrown tendencies and behavioural patterns will be a constant source of trouble within a fellowship.

Constantly influenced by the world

It is not just the past, however. Part of the trouble is that we are constantly being influenced by such attitudes throughout our life in the world now. We are here to influence the world but the world also influences us, and unless we are alert to it, this goes on unnoticed and we find ourselves gradually becoming more worldly in our thinking and behaviour.

This process goes on in many different ways. Many Christians live with unbelieving families, most have unbelieving relatives. We should not cut ourselves off from these. But we are foolish if we do not recognise that people we love and care for very much, and who love and care for us, may sometimes draw our hearts away from God's will and into attitudes which are quite inconsistent with it. It was love and care for Christ which made Peter protest so much that Jesus would never go to the cross (Matthew 16:21-23). Jesus saw in this both the work of Satan, and also a mind that thought in fallen human terms rather than according to the things of God. Sometimes our best friends can be our worst enemies in this respect.

This is very subtle. Those who love us want us to have the respect they think is our due; humbling self and submitting to others is not part of their code of behaviour. They can't see why we should back down in order to make peace, or why we should be ready to forgive a brother who has clearly offended. To them pride is important. So usually is money, and material things, and putting self and family first. Such an influence and blurring of spiritual issues is a source of trouble and spiritual weakness in the lives of many Christians.

Of course there are other influences too. The people among whom we work, and the ethical standards that we are expected to operate with, are very often far from honest and straightforward. The influence of the media and advertising is very strong, and TV is one of the foremost influences in bringing the standards and attitudes of the world into the home and the mind. The lyrics of popular songs leave their message in the mind almost subliminally.

In 1 Corinthians 15:33 Paul pointedly says, 'Do not be misled: "Bad company corrupts good character."' His point is unanswerable. We are bound to be influenced by those amongst whom we spend a great deal of time. Duty requires us at times to be in bad company; maybe for quite long periods of time. Be watchful then; and remember that God protects and keeps those who are alert and prayerful when such company is a matter of duty. But beware of such company—including the company of those you meet through the TV screen—when neither duty nor providence requires your presence.

Romans 12:2 is vital, 'Do not conform any longer to the pattern of this world, but be transformed by the renewing of your mind. Then you will be able to test and approve what God's will is—his good, pleasing and perfect will.' That gives us the antidote to worldly thinking: the mind renewed, resulting in a transformation of thought and attitude so that in experience the will of God is discovered to be good and acceptable and perfect.

An important difference

There is, however, a vital difference between worldly thinking and the use of reason and common-sense. The mind with all its remarkable powers is a creation and gift of God. It is intended to be used for daily life. We must not misunderstand what the Bible says about the will of God to mean that we simply read off God's will from the Bible and do it without needing to think at all. Unfortunately there are Christians who do act in this sort of way. They despise reason and the use of the mind and they look for rules which will cover every eventuality in life and which can simply be obeyed. As Scripture evidently does not give these they deduce rules from what it does give us, and often tend to look on these as having as much authority as what Scripture explicitly says. Such people can cause an enormous amount of trouble within churches. Unfortunately their whole approach and attitude is very similar to that of the Pharisees of Christ's day, and like them they can become very judgmental.

The Bible does not throw any doubt on the value of the mind. What it does is to show that the mind can be used either as it is informed and guided by worldly and unbelieving principles, or else it can be renewed and function according to the principles of Scripture under the guidance of the Holy Spirit. It is this godly use of the mind which is so necessary and important for us.

The Bible shows us that even unbelievers can at times be expected to use their minds to come to proper conclusions. Our Lord said to the multitudes in Luke 12:57, 'Why don't you judge for yourselves what is right?' God had provided them with a faculty of judgment and discernment and Christ rebukes them for their failure to understand the times in which they lived. In Romans 2:4 Paul has Jewish people in mind when he says, 'Or do you show contempt for the riches of his kindness, tolerance and patience, not realising that God's kindness leads you towards repentance?' They ought to have known this. They had the revelation of God in the Old Testament, but they also had minds which should have told them this truth about the kindness of God. In 1 Corinthians 11:14 Paul is writing to Christians but he says to them, 'Does not the very nature of things teach you that if a man has long hair, it is a disgrace to him?'

Using the mind is not necessarily the mark of worldly people. Quite the reverse, one of the marks of the worldly person is that he doesn't think, rather he is impulsive and much more likely to be guided by emotion or popular sentiment than by a mind that has carefully thought things through. A great deal of the Bible consists of examples, illustrations and principles, and these have to be applied with spiritual wisdom to life and the work and direction of the local church. To think purely in human terms is one thing, and leads to trouble; but the answer is not to give up thinking, but rather to bring every thought into subjection to Jesus Christ and to think in a scriptural and spiritual way. Believers have the mind of Christ (1 Corinthians 2:16).

THE DEVIL

Opposition and persecution

The early believers suffered from various forms of opposition and persecution as the pages of the New Testament make very clear. From one point of view this sprang from the world (see John 15:18-20; 17:14), but from a deeper perspective it is attributed to the work of the devil. So for example in Revelation 2:10 the letter to the church at Smyrna says, 'I tell you, the devil will put some of you in prison to test you, and you will suffer persecution for ten days.' The devil was not going to do this directly, rather he would be using the authorities to carry out his purpose. Behind the persecuting authorities of those days Christians were taught to see the hatred and malicious designs of Satan. Similarly in 1 Peter 5:8,9 Peter writes, 'Be self-controlled and alert. Your enemy the devil prowls around like a roaring lion looking for someone to devour. Resist him, standing firm in the faith, because you know that your brothers throughout the world are undergoing the same kind of sufferings.' Only a brief glance at this letter will show us that it was written to Christians who were suffering (see 1:6), and that a great deal of this was persecution of various sorts for Christ's sake (for example 2:18-21).

Not only does the devil incite godless authorities and others to opposition he also tries to exploit it for his own ends. People react to opposition and threat in different ways. Peter himself, who once considered his faith so firm, denied his Lord under the stress of fear. This can be a source of division and strife and has often proved to be in the history of God's people. When some in a church stand firm while others compromise in various ways or even deny the faith it brings all sorts of strains among the members. Some think those who in a moment of weakness denied the faith should be put out of fellowship, and those who avoided trouble by compromise should be disciplined. Others believe a softer line should be taken, and greater allowance made for those weaker in the faith.

Most of us do not face the sort of persecution which the early believers, and many of our contemporaries, have had to experience. However we are subject to opposition of various sorts, and even in our much easier circumstances differences of temperament and differences of spirituality and firmness of faith mean there is tremendous potential for tensions and strains developing within churches. Even with such an ordinary matter as door-to-door visiting a church can be divided into the 'keen types' who get involved in it, and the rest who feel, and are often made to feel, somewhat second-rate Christians because they do not, for whatever reason. A wiser attitude might suggest that people are different, that they have different capabilities and aptitudes, and that all should serve in various ways in the church without unnecessary comparisons being made between the types of service people are involved in.

Watch out for the various ways in which the devil tries to make mischief in churches through the opposition, suffering and trials that God's people go through. The weak often need support not criticism; those who seem to be buckling under pressure are sometimes under much more stress than most realise, especially those tempted to criticise them. Those who are strong in resisting temptation and who can laugh in the face of ridicule or obvious antipathy sometimes have weaknesses in other areas. They may, for example, have great difficulty in being sympathetic and showing sensitivity to those passing through trials. Those who have never known a day's illness find it hard to understand those who scarcely have a day free from pain. The fact is we need each other, and we can be a strength and support to each other. Resisting the devil, in this case, means watching out for his attempts to exploit circumstances in the church and making sure we do all we can to prevent him making trouble.

False teachers

Paul anticipates that visiting the Corinthians might be a very unhappy experience. This is what he says, 'For I am afraid that when I come, I may not find you as I want you to be, and you may not find me as you want me to be. I fear that there may be quarrelling, jealousy, outbursts of anger, factions, slander, gossip, arrogance and disorder' (2 Corinthians 12:20). What reason does he have for anticipating such a catalogue of unpleasantness?

The main problem at Corinth was the presence of false teachers in the church. These appear to have been people who came from elsewhere but who found a ready ear and sphere of operations in Corinth. Paul's concern over these people can be seen in the previous chapter, 'But I am afraid that just as Eve was deceived by the serpent's cunning, your minds may somehow be led astray from your sincere and pure devotion to Christ. For if someone comes to you and preaches a Jesus other than the Jesus we preached, or if you receive a different spirit from the one you received, or a different gospel from the one you accepted, you may put up with it easily enough' (11:3,4). 'For such men are false apostles, deceitful workmen, masquerading as apostles of Christ. And no wonder, for Satan himself masquerades as an angel of light. It is not surprising, then, if his servants masquerade as servants of righteousness. Their end will be what their actions deserve' (vv.13-15).

Here we are presented with the activity of the devil through teachers who appear to be teachers of Christian truth, but who in fact not only bring a different Jesus, and a different gospel, but are themselves only masquerading as servants of righteousness. They had obviously won over a significant number of the people in the church at Corinth. At the same time the rest of the letter shows that Paul had been greatly encouraged when he met Titus who had been to Corinth (7:13-16), so there were obviously also many in the church who appreciated his ministry and recognised his apostleship. In these circumstances he could see that if he went to Corinth the likelihood was that great controversy would be stirred up in the congregation! Hence his fears in 12:20. He knew if he went he would have to confront the false teachers. He knew he would have to call on the church to take sides; to reject the teachers and their teaching, and embrace again with full-hearted assurance the truths of the gospel which he had originally taught them. It was a daunting prospect, but he did not shrink from it; 'I already gave you a warning when I was with you the second time. I now repeat it while absent: On my return I will not spare those who sinned earlier or any of the others' (13:2).

Just as false teachers were the cause of great trouble and division in Corinth, so today their effects in many churches are just as serious. One of the differences is that we do not have apostles to identify such people or refute them with authority (though, of course, not every believer was willing to listen to the apostles in their day). False teachers have all the facilities of the modern media at their fingertips, with the result that there is a profusion of books, videos, cassettes and courses available which are all marketed with maximum skill to make them as attractive as possible. So the devil has a field day, and unless Christians and the churches are established in the faith and vigilant, the potential for confusion, argument and divisiveness is almost endless.

We have in mind errors like those concerning the Bible; the denial of its full inspiration and inerrancy, its authority over every area of life, and its sufficiency; the adding of other authorities to the Bible, especially that of modern-day prophecy, which has probably been the error which has had the most serious effect within the churches during the last twenty years or so. In fact it is not possible to begin to list all the serious errors which circulate in these days, and which can often be found in books on sale in Christian bookshops. From all directions; from liberalism, from sacramentalism, from extreme Pentecostalism, from the cults, from humanism, a never-ending stream of errors and harmful influences seems to flow into the churches.

The result of all this is that Christians get very confused. They are unsettled about the teaching they receive from their pastor because the book they have been reading seems to say almost the opposite. A group of Christians within a church gets very interested in one idea or emphasis and starts to try and push it at every opportunity. Members go off to a great convention or meeting and get swept off their feet and either they insist on the church accepting all that they have come to feel is vital or else they leave and form their own group. The result is argument and dissension, and often division. The worship of God gets forgotten; the need for evangelism and gospel-preaching gets lost in infighting and people trying to get their view to prevail; truth is pushed into a secondary position because no-one seems to be able to discover what it is; and love and peace are the great casualties at the end. Just what the devil ordered!

Evil attitudes

The devil is also behind many of the evil attitudes that so damage relationships between Christians and spoil the harmony within churches. For example Ephesians 4:26,27 says, '"In your anger do not sin." Do not let the sun go down while you are still angry, and do not give the devil a foothold.' There are two possibilities in understanding those words. Firstly, anger gives an opportunity to the devil. Where believers harbour anger the devil sees a real opportunity to stir up trouble in relationships with others and to spoil love within a church. Secondly it could be that not watching out for anger and confessing it at the end of the day gives an opportunity for the devil to stir it up within the heart. Perhaps both are intended here, certainly they can both be combined. The important point is that the devil can both stir up and exploit evil attitudes, and we must therefore be on our guard against them.

There is also a rather remarkable verse in Revelation 2:24 which speaks about some within the church at Thyatira having known 'the depths of Satan' (NKJV). This awful description suggests that some in the church felt it was necessary for them to have known these depths, perhaps using a false sort of reasoning like this; 'how can you help people in the depths of Satan unless you have been there yourself?' There is a similar line of reasoning which is sometimes used in these days also. It argues that Christians need to know all about the world if they going to be able to help people whom they wish to save from it. It also adds that we need to know a great deal about the devil if we are going to understand and help those who are involved in demonic activities. There may be some truth in this attitude, but the great danger is that people within the church get caught up with all the evil things around them. They may become fascinated with demonic power and deception and bring into the church all sorts of unhelpful emphases which end up doing the opposite of what was intended. Instead of the church being better equipped to reach people enslaved to sin and Satan, the very members of the church themselves become ensnared and minds and hearts are opened to evil influence.

His purposes

As far as he can the devil wishes to hinder and frustrate the purpose of God. Ultimately of course this is a vain hope. Nevertheless he can hinder the work of the gospel in certain respects, and he is keen to do so. Paul says, 'For we wanted to come to you—certainly I, Paul, did, again and again—but Satan stopped us' (1 Thessalonians 2:18). How strange! Paul's desire was to visit Thessalonica in order to help and support the believers who had only recently been converted and were suffering quite considerable persecution. Without doubt God overruled in this matter, but Satan stopped Paul from visiting them.

The devil also desires to keep his own empire safe. So we read in 2 Corinthians 4:4, 'The god of this age has blinded the minds of unbelievers, so that they cannot see the light of the gospel of the glory of Christ, who is the image of God.' It is likely that Paul writes this because he was criticised by some at Corinth for not being very successful in his gospel preaching; here is his explanation. In this case the devil blinded the minds of unbelievers, but if he can divert the churches from preaching the gospel, if he can get the members to spend their time fighting amongst each other, that will serve his purpose just as well, if not better.

In fact it probably does serve his purpose better because this also tends to bring churches and hence the name of Christ into disrepute, something he is certainly anxious to do. Christians have been saved to glorify God, and the churches should glorify Father and Son and be models in the community of the difference the grace of God makes to relationships. If the devil can make them hotbeds of backbiting, suspicion and divisiveness then he certainly will do; and if he does then the name of God will be dragged in the mud and greatly dishonoured.

QUESTIONS FOR STUDY AND DISCUSSION

1.In what senses does the New Testament use the word 'world'?

2.How much should the devil be blamed for trouble in the church?

3.What are the biblical marks of 'false teachers'?

4.How does the Bible help us respond to Satan's attacks?

5.Case study: What does 2 Corinthians 2:5-11 teach us about Satan's activity in church relationships?

Part III

Leaders and followers

Perhaps the simplest definition of a leader is "Someone whom people follow". However this may seem rather disconcerting. Think of a person leading a group in mountainous countryside. He comes to some difficult terrain; he works out a way between the rocks and hazards which seems safe; he feels he ought to go ahead and lead the way, so off he sets. After a while he looks back to see how the rest of the group are doing and he finds that someone has seen how to avoid all the difficulties and they are some distance away skirting the problem area, and they will soon be ahead of him in the direction they are going. He may be the leader but no-one is following him; in the circumstances he will probably feel rather foolish.

On the other hand consider a similar sort of scene. The weather is bad; low cloud, poor visibility, continuous rain. The going is steep, rocky and slippery; the group is reasonably large; the leader feels a great sense of responsibility. He often looks round, tries to ensure that all are keeping together, no-one is getting left behind, no-one is too tired to continue. If he is clearly guiding the group safely and his concern for them all is quite apparent, it is likely they will follow him closely, though he may still have to ensure that this is true of everyone. Leadership is not just a matter of appointment or even of training, it is a combination of the confidence which those who follow feel and the concern which the leader shows.

Before turning to the New Testament a glance at leadership in the Old Testament is worthwhile. The monarchy in Israel was very different from what is to be expected in churches, yet it has some valuable reminders. For example, the division that took place between Judah in the south, and Israel in the north, came about because of the foolishness of Rehoboam (1 Kings 12:1-24). Rehoboam rejected the advice of the elders who had served his father Solomon, advice based on long experience. Instead he followed the advice of the young men who had grown up with him and who served him. This act of folly split the one people of God into two for the rest of their history, a division which is only overcome in Christ Jesus.

Both David and Solomon relied heavily on a small group of men for the administration of their kingdom (see 2 Samuel 8:15-17; 1 Kings 4:1-6).

Three things could be noted about David's reign and his relations with other leaders. Firstly, one of his closest advisers and friend, Ahithophel, turned traitor and joined in with Absalom's rebellion (2 Samuel 15:12,31). It was probably this treachery that led David to write Psalm 41:9 and 55:20,21. Such breakdowns of trust and loyalty are not unknown in church leaderships today.

Secondly, although Joab remained loyal for the larger part of David's reign and David clearly looked upon him as indispensable, David was never able to control the crueller and more self-centred aspects of Joab's character. It is certainly surprising to hear the conqueror of Goliath saying, 'And today, though I am the anointed king, I am weak, and these sons of Zeruiah are too strong for me' (2 Samuel 3:39). Joab was quite prepared to act on his own initiative contrary to David's known wishes. He was the hard man in David's leadership team. How you deal with the maverick who is only out for truth and righteousness, so he maintains, is one of the ongoing difficulties for leaderships.

Finally, David, fine warrior and man of faith that he was, could also be lamentably weak. Not only was this so with Joab, but particularly with his sons Amnon (he was furious with him [2 Samuel 13:21] but does not seem to have done anything about his sin) and Absalom. The wisdom which he showed when he served Saul seems to have deserted him when it came to his own family. One of the values of advisers and shared leadership is that the strengths of some can compensate for the weaknesses of others. This only works if there is frank and honest co-operation together.

Chapter 6

Leadership and ministry

W hen Paul writes to the church in Philippi he addresses his letter "to all the saints in Christ Jesus…, together with the overseers and deacons." This is the only letter which includes the leaders of a church in its greeting. There are good grounds for thinking that it was generally the case for New Testament churches to have overseers and deacons. Writing to Timothy about leadership in the church, he also refers to overseers and deacons (I Timothy 3; overseers in verses 1-7, and deacons in verses 8-13). The clear implication of this is that Paul expected Timothy to be involved in teaching the church at Ephesus about what kind of person would be suitable for these positions, and perhaps to be involved in the process of setting them apart for their ministry.

LEADERS IN THE CHURCH

The traditional word for 'overseer' is 'bishop', but this is unsuitable as the word is used in a quite different way today. The word 'deacon' might be better translated as 'servant'. This would mean that both words would have a functional content, as in the Greek, 'overseers and servants'. It is not quite clear what understanding we should have of 'servant'; does he serve the church, or does he serve God on behalf of and in the interests of the church? My understanding is that deacons serve the church, they attend to its needs and minister to its members in a whole variety of ways. If Acts 6:1-6 is to be thought of as providing an example of the ministry of deacons, it shows us the men set apart serving the widows and making sure that they were all provided for. If a deacon is to be thought of as a servant of the church then this gives the word a very different flavour to what is usual in churches today.

However the concern of this chapter, and this book, is not primarily with titles, nor with trying to elucidate precisely what forms of church officers we can discern in the New Testament. The fact is that two churches can have both elders and deacons—overseers and servants—and yet the way these two groups function, and are understood, can be quite different. This book is more concerned with the quality of leadership, the way leaders function, and the areas of ministry and care, than with names or titles, or division of labour. So it is more concerned with what is generally seen as the responsibility of elders than with the responsibilities of deacons, but many churches have deacons whose responsibilities are extended to include at least a measure of oversight and pastoral care. In the New Testament itself there is not a sharp demarcation discernible between elders and deacons. For this reason we shall continue to speak primarily about 'leaders'.

At the same time it is important to consider the significance of titles that are used for leaders in the New Testament. The term 'overseer' obviously suggest a watchful care of the church and a superintendence of its worship and work (cf. Hebrews 13:17). The term 'pastor' is used in Ephesians 4:11, though it is difficult to know why 'pastor' is used rather than the literal 'shepherd'. The term 'pastor' and the adjective 'pastoral' have become very popular, perhaps rightly so in view of the use of shepherd imagery in the Bible. 'Pastor' seems a nice title; 'shepherd' might appear rather odd, but it is the responsibility of shepherding, the spiritual function that the word 'pastor' conveys. That is the important thing.

In the same verse 'teacher' occurs. At least the function of teacher is obvious, but the verse is not exactly clear. Are pastors and teachers two offices, or are there some who are 'pastors and teachers', one group of men who fulfil both of these functions? Or does it mean those who pastor, or shepherd, by teaching; understanding the 'and' not as a connective but as explanatory of pastors? Important though these questions are, for our purpose it is enough to see that teaching is an essential part of leadership in a church.

Another term that the New Testament uses is 'elder', a term which is clearly interchangeable with overseer (1 Peter 5:1,2; Titus 1:5-7). The word 'elder' has a history in the Old Testament and Judaism, but was also widely used in the Graeco-Roman world in which the early churches were planted. It is not therefore a very specific word and points to the maturity and wisdom which are particularly associated with age and experience. It points to men who are respected, who have a sense of responsibility and can be entrusted with decision-making and judgments. The word 'leader' is also used (Hebrews 13:7,17), and the idea is also present in 1 Timothy 5:17—translated in the NIV 'direct the affairs of the church', rather a paraphrase but giving a good idea of what is meant by 'leading'.

There are other more descriptive words used in the New Testament. The word 'minister', which also has been used widely in recent days, is too general to refer to any particular office. 'Minister of the Word' is a description of the task of preaching and teaching. 'Minister' usually translates the same word as 'deacon', so it carries the idea of service. 'Preacher' or 'herald' is more specific and has the idea of authoritative proclamation. In the New Testament, preachers were often itinerants. Apostles could be preachers; so also, presumably, could evangelists and prophets. Certainly they engaged in authoritative proclamation of the gospel. While the word 'preacher' is not used of any office in the local church, this doesn't mean that there was no preaching there, nor that one or more in leadership were not involved in this work. It does seem to suggest, however, that leadership in the church is more concerned with the care and nurture of believers, while preaching has more of an evangelistic edge to it. 1 Timothy 5:17 speaks of those 'who labour in word and teaching'—this is a rather literalistic rendering which avoids putting an interpretative gloss on the translation. This verse shows conclusively that some elders, if not all, have their primary work as the teaching of the Word of God.

Paul, James, Peter and Jude all describe themselves as 'slaves' of Jesus Christ (Paul does so in Philippians 1:1; 'slaves' as opposed to 'servants' in v.2; see also Romans 1:1; Titus 1:1; James 1:1; 2 Peter 1:1; Jude 1:1. In Titus Paul says 'a slave of God', while James says 'a slave of God' and the Lord Jesus Christ.) This emphasis is a very important one. Leaders have a position of rule and ministry in the church, but they exercise this ministry as slaves of Christ. It would be true to the New Testament to see all believers as slaves to Christ, for he has purchased us all, and we are all to do his will and serve him. Nevertheless the call to leadership involves a special call from Christ through the church, and those in leadership need to have a particular sense of being willing slaves to do his will. On the one hand this gives them a sense of independence from the church. Even though they may be remunerated by the church, they are primarily appointed by the Lord Jesus Christ and are answerable to him. They are not the slaves of people, even Christian people, they stand or fall to their master. On the other hand this must mean a certain humility and faithfulness. Leaders do not always look or sound very much like slaves of Christ. Consider 1 Corinthians 3:5;

4:1, where 'servant' is not the same word as 'slave' but the thought is much the same: 'What, after all, is Apollos? And what is Paul? Only servants, through whom you came to believe, as the Lord assigned to each his task.' 'So then, men ought to regard us as servants of Christ and as those entrusted with the secret things of God.'

Two other questions arise at this point. Firstly, are there office-bearers in the New Testament churches? That is to say, did the New Testament churches have distinct offices occupied by those set apart to fill the office and fulfil its functions? This question does not necessarily admit of an easy answer. It is uncertain whether deacons have a specific office. There are certainly people set apart to serve in the church, but their functions could well be very diverse and it is easy to envisage those set apart for various ministries never meeting together as 'deacons'; they simply 'deacon'—that is, minister, serve, according to the responsibility given to them. There are far more grounds for considering elders/overseers as occupying an office, but even here a note of caution should be struck. The main emphasis seems to be on function—leaders are above all func-tionaries; they are not like a board of directors, they *work* in the church. They are fully involved in taking the lead in the church's ministries. Does 'elder' actually cover several offices—pastor, teacher, preacher, evangelist? This also is not certain. 1 Timothy 5:17 probably divides elders into those who rule and those who minister the word by teaching, but even this cannot be proved. The New Testament emphasis does seem to be on a group of leaders in the church and we must turn next to the question of the plurality of elders.

Should every church have a plurality of elders? Granted that the word is generally used in the plural, was plurality a matter of principle or simply a matter of coincidence? One thing that seems clear is that most of the churches that we know about were considerably larger than most churches today. After all there was only one church in each place. Was there a plurality of elders because large churches needed this? In the early days the churches had no buildings of their own to meet in. Was it possible for churches of thousands of members—as the Jerusalem church—to meet together as we do, at least for regular worship? Were the churches in houses (e.g. Colossians 4:15; Philemon 2) sub-groups within the main church which met together regularly for ministry and instruction because the church was too big for all its members to gather together in one place? Isn't it inevitable that in the New Testament situation most churches would have had a plurality of elders? Does that, however, mean that a church today of, say, thirty members ought on principle to have several elders? Such a proposition seems ridiculous, and is sure to lead to all sorts of difficulties. To have elders who have nothing to do in the church except to meet with other elders seems a complete misunderstanding of what spiritual leadership is all about, and is likely to be a recipe for disaster.

All this leads to the conclusion that the New Testament allows for variation and flexibility. To say that churches should have elders and deacons is surely correct, but there is room for variation in how they are organised and how they function. The important thing is that the functions are carried out and the work they are needed for is done.

LEADERSHIP RESPONSIBILITIES

Having considered briefly the leadership terms in the New Testament we can consider what the functions of leaders are. Instead of looking at these in detail we shall simply consider broad categories. The main point is that for relations within the church to be harmonious and for the church to do its work, these functions must be carried out.

Ministry of the Word

It is quite clear that within any church there must be a proper ministry of the Word of God. This is not simply a matter of the Bible being preached, it is much more than that. It means that there must be an effective application of the Word of God to every area of the church's life, to all the members, and to all the varied trials and problems they have to face. It is possible to have good Bible ministry on Sundays and yet for the structure, ordering and carrying out of the church's different ministries to owe more to business practice than anything else, and for the counselling of members and the resolution of their problems to rely on secular theories of psycho-therapy rather than on biblical principles. The leaders must ensure that God's Word *rules* in the church, that it is the first resource and ultimate authority for all that the church does. This is not necessarily a matter of finding proof texts to justify everything that is done, though plain texts should not be despised as they are sometimes apt to be. Rather it means that the principles which inform decisions, the attitudes shown, and the manner in which the church goes about its business, all arise out of the Word of God.

Several things follow from this. The first is that leaders must themselves be Bible students. They must have an above average knowledge of the Bible; they must be continually developing their understanding; and they must learn how to apply the Bible to church life—to situations, to problems, to people, to service. They need to be reading books based on the Bible which deal with practical questions of ministry. Ideally it would be good if leaders could meet together to discuss and consider various aspects of ministry in the light of God's Word. One leader might be delegated to read a book, and then review and summarise it as an introduction to a discussion on the subject with which it deals. In our modern, complex society it is a never-ending task to keep abreast of all the questions that require godly consideration and informed answers.

That, however, is only preparatory to the main task which is to bring what is learnt to bear upon the life and work of the church. There never seems to be enough time or opportunity to deal with this adequately. Consider one area of work briefly—the teaching and nurturing of young people in the church. They are exposed to the influence of the media, to the pressure of their peers and probably to secular humanism at school. The Sunday School teachers and young people's leaders struggle to get programmes which will interest and keep them—that is often the first priority. But what the young people need is Bible teaching that is relevant, understandable and interesting, which will actually help them and mould their lives for the future. Church leaders have a ministry first to those involved in the young people's work, and to parents within the congregation. Those who work with the young people (one or two of whom may be included in the leadership of the church) will often need help, and will certainly need encouragement and pastoral care. Yet this must not be given in an oppressive way; workers must know they are given space to take responsibility and take their own decisions (within agreed limits), yet they must feel that the leaders are behind them, support them, pray for them and are always ready with encouragement, guidance and biblical wisdom as these are needed. And young people's work is only one area of the church's ministry!

So the work of ministering the Word is not just a matter of preaching or Bible Studies—though these are of crucial importance, of course. Leaders must learn to think biblically so that they can counsel and guide biblically. A great deal is communicated in personal conversation. Leaders need to be able to reflect biblical principles and priorities when they are simply talking informally, or when there is no studied attempt at giving advice or answering a question or solving a problem. It is no good for leaders to be able to give the right answer when they have thought about the question and studied the Bible upon it, if in their general conversation they reflect the worldly attitudes into which we all find it so easy to fall.

A great many problems and divisions arise because of a lack of thorough Bible ministry. Most of the difficulties met with in church life arise because Christians do not know how to handle the Bible, do not study it thoroughly, and are not prepared to let it settle matters of dispute. They too often put down every view except their own as "just your interpretation"! The only answer to all this is regular, careful explanation of the Bible, which not only directly instructs but also sets a pattern for understanding and using the Bible.

Pastoral care

This cannot be divorced from the ministry of the Word because pastoral care includes the application of the Word to all the different sorts and conditions found within the church. We are really looking at the same thing from a different perspective. Pastoral care begins not with the Bible, but with people. Shepherds care for the flock, and the sheep who make it up; leaders watch over the souls of those entrusted to their care (Hebrews 13:17; cf. Luke 2:8). The words in Hebrews and Luke are interesting. Leaders are to keep awake in order to watch over souls. The shepherds outside Bethlehem camped out in the fields so that they could guard their flocks. On the one hand there is the thought of watching out for problems and needs, guarding and protecting; on the other there is the thought of wakefulness, discomfort and dedication to the task. The sheep may sleep; the shepherds must be awake!

We are now touching on a point which is crucial for the harmony of the church. Quarrels, factions and divisions are nearly always the result of a failure in pastoral care. This point has already been discussed in some detail; here the moral is drawn: there must be proper pastoral care within the church. This is the responsibility of leaders. Here the question of the plurality of elders can arise again. It has been suggested, partly on the basis of Exodus 18:21, that one man can adequately care for about ten families. It has also been suggested that a full-time pastor can cope with a church of up to about one hundred members, above that number the church will need another man full-time in the work. These figures are arbitrary, and circumstances differ widely. A church made up of a hundred well-taught, mature believers is one thing; just ten recent converts with many spiritual, moral and social problems can be more than enough for one man. Moreover men have different capabilities and capacities.

When we bring together what is needed for a thorough-going ministry of the Word and adequate pastoral care, a figure of much more than a hundred members means a load difficult to be borne by just one man. Of course it will not usually be the case that a man is totally alone, most will have others associated with him in leadership, whatever they may be called and however the functions of ministry are divided among them. However, in Acts 6:4 the apostles said, 'We will *devote ourselves* to prayer and the ministry of the word' (the same word as is used in 2:42). Taken in conjunction with 1 Timothy 4:13 this suggests men whose priority in life, if not full-time occupation, was prayer and the ministry of the Word. Leadership in a church ideally requires those who are committed to the work full-time, and this seems to have been the case in New Testament days. Although the pastoral load can be shared with those who bear some of it in a part-time capacity, and many elders and deacons have given valiant service in this way, it is quite clear if we consider what is involved in leadership that this is not satisfactory once a church has reached a certain size. One man may be able to fulfil most of the obligations of ministry of the Word, but he will not be able to fulfil all the obligations of pastoral care, and at that point the church should look for an additional pastor to assist in the work as a colleague.

Chapter 6

Spiritual direction

Another important element in leadership is giving spiritual direction to the church. It is possible for this to be taken too far. Analogies taken from armies or businesses are not always helpful. A church cannot set targets or determine goals in the way other organisations do. But churches have functions and are aiming for certain results and so the leaders are to give direction and a sense of purpose, both to the whole membership as a body, and to the individual members as well. Many churches seem to have no real sense of purpose and no vision about what they ought to be accomplishing. Members are content to attend Sunday by Sunday, various activities are carried out in a reasonably satisfactory manner, there may be conversions from time to time, so what else can be expected or be done?

Spiritual direction is first of all concerned with the spiritual life of the church and its members. The ultimate goal for all believers is conformity to Jesus Christ; we are to grow like him, and we are to grow like him together. So the ministry is not just concerned with faithfully explaining Scripture, it is concerned with seeing growth and development on the part of all the members. This means there has to be prayerful and sensitive planning of ministry. Are all the different aspects of Scripture and the life of godliness being covered? Is there a balance between Old Testament and New Testament? Is real practical help being given to believers as they face many different challenges and difficulties in their everyday lives? Is the leadership even aware of the sort of problems that members are facing and struggling with? These are only a small sample of the questions that arise when the matter of spiritual direction is considered.

Spiritual direction applies to many areas of church life. Are the resources of the church being used to best advantage? Are the various activities being carried out because they have been established for a long time, or because they are meeting a need, fulfilling a function which is vital for the life or witness of the church? Does the church have a sense of purpose in the area where the Lord has placed it? Does it have a sense of responsibility to befriend people in the neighbourhood and to bring the gospel to them in the most thoughtful and suitable ways? Does it try to reach out in different ways in order to reach different sorts of people? Does it have any sort of strategy for reaching people around it? Churches may answer questions like these in slightly different ways, that is their privilege and responsibility under the leading of the Holy Spirit. Leaders, however, must be aware of such questions—and many more—and must give a spiritual, well-thought out lead to the members. Habit and drift can become real enemies of a church's vitality and usefulness and leaders must have their eyes open to this.

Spheres of ministry

It is often assumed that leaders are all expected to function in much the same way, preachers in one way, of course, elders in another and deacons another again. It may well be, however, that responsibilities and functions should be much more shared out among leaders according to the gifts which they have. Many leaders just "lead" in a very undefined way. They attend the appropriate meeting, pray about the work, make their verbal contributions, but that may well be all. Usually, however, the personalities, temperaments and abilities of the various leaders differ quite considerably. God has made them different people and given them different gifts. In these circumstances it seems appropriate that each leader should have those responsibilities for which he is best suited. One may be suited for work with young people, one may have gifts of personal conversation and counselling, another have evangelistic gifts, another administrative gifts, another the ability to lead Bible studies, another gets on well with older people. Perhaps this is enough to make the point. While there should be general oversight of all the church's work and witness by those called to leadership, there can be more specific oversight of areas of work by those who are prepared by God for such responsibility.

BIBLICAL LEADERSHIP

Examples, not lords

Peter writes, 'Be shepherds of God's flock that is under your care, serving as overseers—not because you must, but because you are willing, as God wants you to be, not greedy for money, but eager to serve, not lording it over those entrusted to you, but being examples to the flock' (1 Peter 5:2,3). While all he says here is of the greatest importance, the focus for the moment is on the last of the contrasts that Peter uses. 'Lording it over those entrusted to you', is a very expressive phrase. Nearly all of us would secretly like to be lords; to have power and influence; to have authority over others. Many have no chance of getting into any position like that in secular employment, but in the church it is different. There is far less competition, for a start; many churches are crying out for leaders. Probably very few ever covet leadership positions because they want power, but having got into such a position, they are open to temptation along that line.

Peter says this is not the way oversight is to be exercised within a church. Leaders are not to be tyrants; there is to be no heavy-handed authoritarianism; they are not to domineer. Wayne Grudem says in his commentary on 1 Peter (*Tyndale New Testament Commentary, IVP*), 'The word [lording] always seems to involve bringing something into subjection by the use of force, whether physical, military, or political. Here Peter forbids the use of arbitrary, arrogant, selfish, or excessively restrictive rule. He implies that elders should govern not by the use of threats, emotional intimidation, or flaunting of power, nor generally by the use of 'political' force within the church, but rather by power of example whenever possible.' Important though the negative is, and in days of indiscipline such as today the danger of authoritarianism is very real, it is the positive which we consider here. After all, it is the exercise of the positive qualities which will negate the negative.

In what ways are leaders to be examples to the flock? Presumably in every area of the Christian life, but some things seem essential to say. Leaders, firstly, must be examples in godliness. The qualities needed for elders and deacons as spelled out by Paul in 1 Timothy 3 show this very clearly. Gifts are scarcely hinted at; the emphasis is on Christian character, people whose lives are exemplary! This is foundational for leadership in a church of Jesus Christ. Of course, no-one is perfect, nor do church members expect leaders who are perfect. But they do expect leaders who have godliness as their goal, who are pursuing it, and progressing in it. Some leaders are younger in age than others. Paul said to Timothy, 'Don't let anyone look down on you because you are young, but set an example for the believers in speech, in life, in love, in faith and in purity.' (1 Timothy 4:12). The way in which Timothy was to prevent believers looking down on him because of his youth, or despising his ministry, was not by adopting a superior attitude and asserting his authority, but by the godly example which he set.

Secondly, leaders must set an example in submission to Scripture. The whole church is under the Word of God, and leaders minister by the Word of God. It is therefore essential that they show submission themselves to that Word. Unfortunately this is not always apparent. Prejudice, tradition, the way in which we've always done it, what worked well enough in the past, everyone's doing it this way now—these things can exert an undue influence upon leaders just as much as upon other Christians. Leaders should be seen to be people who are consciously seeking to obey Scripture in their personal lives. They should be people who are searching the Scripture and trying to apply biblical principles to their great responsibility in leadership. They should be proactive in considering the life and work of the church in the light of God's Word, rather than reluctantly reactive when someone brings Scripture to their attention. And they should welcome those who have a concern to bring all the church's life into conformity to Scripture, and always be open to persuasion from the Word.

It has already been admitted that leaders are not perfect, nor will they ever be so. It is therefore very important that they should set an example in repentance, apology and forgiveness. The importance of these things for the harmony of the church has already been stressed. Knowing how crucial they are, leaders must be sure to set an example here. However, there is a problem. Leaders often feel it will undermine their authority if they admit to faults and sins. They feel it is rather beneath them to apologise to 'ordinary' or younger members. Of course some sins may unfit them for leadership altogether, but that is not our concern here. Some leaders, and mature members, do indeed set an example of expressing their repentance in the prayer meeting, sometimes bewailing their extreme sinfulness, but it appears that for all their manifold sinfulness there is no-one in the congregation that they actually see the need to apologise to or ask for forgiveness! At its worst this can be nauseous hypocrisy.

The fact is that when leaders take their falls and failures seriously, and are prepared to apologise when this is necessary, sometimes, perhaps, to the whole church, this has a sobering and wholesome effect upon everyone. It shows everyone that such leaders take sin seriously; more seriously in themselves than in other people. It makes people examine their own ways and attitudes; it makes them ask whether there is not some confession they also should make. The public sins of leaders are particularly important.

Consider how Moses and Aaron lost their temper with the Israelites (Numbers 20:9-13). As a result of that neither of them was permitted to enter the land of promise. God said, 'Because you did not trust in me enough to honour me in the sight of the Israelites, you will not bring this community into the land I give them.' Leaders must honour God before those they lead. Harsh words in the church meeting, heated words in leaders' meetings, needed to be quickly repented of, and apologised for. Just as Israel went into the promised land, God's people will receive the blessing he has prepared for them, but without repentance this may not be until there has been a change of pastor or leaders.

Leaders must also set an example in taking their responsibilities seriously. Pastors and leaders sometimes complain of a lack of commitment on the part of Christian people in these days; they feel there is a slackness and casualness abroad which has seeped into the churches. This may well be true, but one of the best ways of combating it is by the example of those in leadership. If they are 'never lacking in zeal, but keep [their] spiritual fervour, serving the Lord' (Romans 12:11), this will have its effect upon the whole membership. In the first place this means setting an example in those duties and responsibilities which lie on them simply as Christians and church members. Example here is very important. What are leaders saying if they are usually late for the various meetings of the church, if they always sit in the back rows of the church, if their voices are seldom heard in the prayer meeting unless they are specifically asked to lead in prayer, if they seldom welcome visitors or converse with a wide variety of members of the congregation, if they virtually never invite anyone to their homes? Rather it is those who set an example in these and many other small matters who should be appointed to leadership. Those who are faithful in smaller matters are the ones who are suited to take on greater responsibilities (see Luke 16:10-12).

In addition leaders should set an example in the fulfilment of the responsibilities which are specifically theirs. There are some responsibilities which all leaders share, there may be some which belong particularly to an individual, there are some which leaders feel particularly suited for, there are others which they find difficult. They must be faithful in carrying out all their responsibilities; not neglecting the ones they don't like and spending all their time on those they enjoy. One of the ways in which dissension easily arises among leaders is when some feel that others are not really pulling their weight, or when a few feel that more difficult and delicate matters, or things which are more mundane and have a low profile in the church, are always being left to them because the others are opting out of them.

It is true that leaders have different abilities and that is why it can be a good thing for responsibilities to be shared out according to gift. In addition all leaders have their limitations, and they need to set an example in being honest about them. Leaders, perhaps especially pastors, sometimes feel they have got to appear to be omni-competent, able to do anything and everything in the church and do it well. In such circumstances they are not ready to face up to their weaknesses (though they may feel them acutely in private), and spend a great deal of time trying to put on a facade which hides the truth. This is ridiculous and overlooks the fact that the Lord has shared out his gifts among his people so that they can work together, and one can supply what another lacks. The unspoken idea that Christ concentrates whole galaxies of gifts on just a few individuals in the church, and all the rest of the members are practically devoid of them, cripples a church and prevents it from functioning as it ought.

If the emphasis in leadership is on example this means that personal qualities will be stressed rather than what might be called positional authority. In other words leaders are followed because of what they are, rather than simply because of the position they hold. Their words are listened to, their advice heeded, their proposals accepted, because the church knows the sort of men they are. It knows they are men of prayer; it knows they are men of the Word; it knows they are not just out for their own position in the church, or simply to get their own ideas accepted. The more leaders are real examples, the more they will be followed; the less they will have to resort to anything that smacks of authoritarianism. That means that there will be a relaxed—in the best sense of the word—atmosphere in the church. Fear and tension will be dissipated. There will not be a 'them and us' attitude on the part of the members to the leaders, or vice versa. When tensions and differences do arise, as of course they will, it will be much easier to approach them and resolve them.

The eastern shepherd did not drive his flock, employing dogs to snap at the heels of the sheep to keep them going in the right direction, but went before them, leading them in the right way, and the sheep followed him. This is an extraordinarily high ideal for leadership, but it is the one the Scripture sets before us. It is one thing to aspire to the title 'Shepherd', 'Pastor', it is quite another thing to have the qualities that belong to a good shepherd. If we are to take seriously the words of the great Shepherd we won't even use titles at all (Matthew 23:8-12), for there is only one real Shepherd. All the emphasis will be on the spiritual graces and qualities which enable leaders to function as they should in the church.

Before leaving this section it might be valuable to point out how frequent the idea of leadership by example is in the New Testament. This is how Paul can speak of himself. 'Follow my example, as I follow the example of Christ' (1 Corinthians 11:1). 'I am not writing this to shame you, but to warn you, as my dear children. Even though you have ten thousand guardians in Christ, you do not have many fathers, for in Christ Jesus I became your father through the gospel. Therefore I urge you to imitate me' (1 Corinthians 4:14-16). 'You yourselves know how you ought to follow our example' (2 Thessalonians 3:7). 'Join with others in following my example, brothers, and take note of those who live according to the pattern we gave you' (Philippians 3:17). Very few leaders would feel able to speak as Paul does, but perhaps that is partly because they are conscious that their example is one that falls far too short of what it ought to be. We must remember that many of Paul's converts were Gentiles who had no idea of what Christian living was all about. In those circumstances it was necessary not only for Paul to teach, but also to model the Christian life for those believers. We are reaching a situation in which this is almost as important today.

Nor is this the end of the New Testament evidence on this subject. In Titus 2:7,8 Paul says, 'In all things set them an example by doing what is good. In your teaching show integrity, seriousness and soundness of speech that cannot be condemned, so that those who oppose you may be ashamed because they have nothing bad to say about us.' All leaders must strive to live in such a way that after they have gone on to glory it may be said of them as of the leaders of the group of Hebrews who received the letter of that name, 'Remember your leaders, who spoke the word of God to you. Consider the outcome of their way of life and imitate their faith' (Hebrews 13:7).

Servants, not managers

Luke 22:24-27 is another crucial passage when considering the Christian concept of leadership. At the passover when Jesus instituted the Lord's Supper we read of the disciples, 'Also a dispute arose among them as to which of them was to be considered greatest. Jesus said to them, "The kings of the Gentiles lord it over them; and those who exercise authority over them call themselves Benefactors. But you are not to be like that. Instead, the greatest among you should be like the youngest, and the one who rules like the one who serves. For who is greater, the one who is at the table or the one who serves? Is it not the one who is at the table? But I am among you as one who serves."' This is very similar in tone and content to Matthew 20:25-28 (see also Mark 9:35).

The importance of this passage is seen in that it was necessary for the Lord to speak these words on two separate occasions; the disciples appear to have been very slow to understand what he was teaching them. On several occasions they disputed about who should be the greatest. Perhaps we do not hear today of such open discussion as this, but it is true that the words, actions and attitudes of some show that this is a matter of importance to them. People can feel slighted when they think they are not being given the position or appreciation which they believe they ought to have in a church. The fact that such a dispute should have taken place on such an occasion as the Lord's Supper and on the night in which he was betrayed, shows us how proud and insensitive the human heart can be, even when it is disciples who are concerned. In this case it was those who had gone out preaching in the name of Jesus and performed miracles in his name.

Even more important are the actual words used by Jesus. He draws a contrast between the Gentiles and his disciples. By the Gentiles he means the pagan, unbelieving world. Leadership, he says, is exercised in one way in the world, but 'you are not to be like that.' Once again the word 'lord', 'lord it over them', is used. There is a certain grim humour in the phrase, 'those who exercise authority over them call themselves Benefactors'. One thinks of certain towns in Northern England where statues are to be found in the town centre, or perhaps a park, of some alderman of ample proportions—'a great benefactor to the people of this town'! One wonders whether it was the ordinary people who erected the statue out of gratitude, or whether it was not his fellow aldermen, councillors and mill owners who did it, or even perhaps if he had it erected himself! 'You are not to be like that.'

We must be clear about this. These words define for us the essence of leadership and greatness amongst Christians. Later words in the epistles do not modify or qualify what our Lord is teaching here. Quite the reverse, all the other instructions about leaders and leadership have to be understood in the light of the great principle enshrined in these words. You cannot be a Pope and a 'Servant of Servants' at the same time. The two things are mutually exclusive. There is no place for little popes in the churches. Leadership means embracing servitude, and a person enters more and more into the spirit of what true greatness is in the service of the Lord, as he forgets things like status, position, authority, influence, power, applause, appreciation, and is found in the church as his Lord, 'one who serves'.

This is a similar concept to that of being 'slaves of Christ'. Here are those who 'rule', but they rule by serving. They are servants of Christ and of the church for his sake. They take their pattern of leadership from Christ himself. However paradoxical it may seem, and however discomfiting to the natural desires they may have, they have to take their cross and die to self, following their Master. When Jesus says, 'the greatest among you should be like the youngest', he means he must take the lowliest place. 'In the ancient world it was accepted that age gave privileges. The youngest was, by definition, the lowliest.' (Leon Morris, *Luke, Tyndale New Testament Commentaries*, IVP; p.308.)

Unfortunately, we very easily think in terms of a hierarchical structure within churches. There are the members, then above them, are the deacons, above them are the elders, with probably the pastor occupying his own little niche as at least 'first among equals'. Just as in secular employment we think of people working their way up the rungs of the ladder, so it becomes very difficult to avoid the same idea within the church. But that is not the whole situation. We often think of young ministers, just out of college, beginning with small churches; probably the thought is that they cannot do as much damage in a small church as they might in a large one! Yet it is usually the case that small churches need men of experience; those who can bring the members together, who can build them up, enthuse them, motivate them for Christian service and outreach. Then the idea is that once a younger man has got a few years experience in a smaller church, has made his mistakes, found his feet, may be is beginning to build the church up, the time is ripe for him to move on to greener pastures and higher ground; in short a larger church. And larger churches, of course, wouldn't even consider calling someone without a proven track record, thus helping to perpetuate the system. And there are other rungs beyond that.

It would be rather easy to parody all this, and to overlook the fact that within churches it is certainly going to look as if there is a hierarchical structure. However, in fact, there is no need for there to be real hierarchy. It all depends upon attitudes and perceptions. Some time ago I saw a business programme on television which looked at this from a business point of view. A typical company structure is usually thought of in hierarchical terms, rather like this:

Managing Director
Manager of dept. Manager of dept. Manager of dept.
employees employees employees employees employees employees

Looked at in this way, especially in terms of authority and salary, we have a pyramid rising to the managing director at the top. But as was pointed out if we think of the situation in terms of responsibility we should really turn the pyramid upside down:

employees employees employees employees employees employees
Manager of dept. Manager of dept. Manager of dept.
Managing Director

There is, surely, a very real sense in which this is the way we ought to think of leadership in the church. The world may look at it in one way but we are to turn that upside down, not just in thought but in reality. In the church those who lead take the responsibility for the whole church and serve all the members. They take the *lowest* place, and the burden is gladly accepted on their shoulders. From one point of view the shepherd may appear to be over the flock, but in fact all that the shepherd does is in the interests of the flock. He serves the flock; some of the sheep possibly causing him a great deal of trouble, hard work, loss of sleep. His concern always is for the welfare of the sheep, he spends and is spent for them.

NECESSARY QUALITIES

What qualities are needed if leaders are going to be true servants of Christ and serve the flock for his sake? Just one or two will be mentioned. The first is love. It is probably easier to be a leader if you do not love, and are not too closely involved with those you lead. What made Paul's relations with the Corinthian church so painful to him was the depth of his love for them; something which comes out again and again in 2 Corinthians, 'For I wrote to you out of great distress and anguish of heart and with many tears, not to grieve you but to let you know the depth of my love for you.' 'Make room for us in your hearts. We have wronged no-one, we have corrupted no-one, we have exploited no-one. I do not say this to condemn you; I have said before that you have such a place in our hearts that we would live or die with you.' 'So I will very gladly spend for you everything I have and expend myself as well. If I love you more, will you love me less?' (2:4; 7:2,3; 12:15). It is this sort of Christ-like quality of love that leaders must have, if they are to serve the flock.

Jesus Christ is a pattern to us of a good shepherd, 'I am the good shepherd. The good shepherd lays down his life for the sheep. The hired hand is not the shepherd who owns the sheep. So when he sees the wolf coming, he abandons the sheep and runs away. Then the wolf attacks the flock and scatters it. The man runs away because he is a hired hand and cares nothing for the sheep' (John 10:11-13). True under-shepherds of Jesus Christ cannot run; it cannot be said of them that they care nothing for the sheep. They are not just appointees; they are not just 'doing a job'; they are not in leadership to boost their self-esteem or gain a reputation; they serve the sheep and put themselves out for the sheep because they love them.

Self-evidently another quality is humility; no-one but the humble person is going to take the lowest place and give himself in selfless service to others. When Jesus Christ called people to come to him, to take his yoke upon them and learn from him, he said, 'For I am gentle and humble in heart and you will find rest for your souls. For my yoke is easy and my burden is light' (Matthew 11:29,30). There is too much leadership which is authoritarian and burdensome, just as that of the scribes and Pharisees was; it leaves people 'weary and burdened.' The contrast between Jesus and the spiritual leaders of the Jews was absolute, 'They tie up heavy loads and put them upon men's shoulders, but they themselves are not willing to lift a finger to move them' (Matthew 23:4). One of the reasons why Jesus was so approachable and the crowds flocked to him, rather than to those who ministered in the synagogues, was surely the fact that, though his teaching was searching and his demands so high, his personal manner was quiet and humble and he welcomed all—children, Gentiles, women, tax collectors and sinners; all but the arrogant and self-righteous, who could not stand him anyway.

Another quality is sympathy. This is also something which the New Testament draws attention to in our Lord Jesus Christ, 'For we do not have a high priest who is unable to sympathise with our weaknesses, but we have one who has been tempted in every way, just as we are—yet was without sin. Let us then approach the throne of grace with confidence, so that we may receive mercy and find grace to help us in our time of need' (Hebrews 4:15,16). The Lord Jesus does not condone sinful weakness, he is grieved when his people fall into temptation, he is ready both to rebuke and correct with discipline when necessary, but he understands our weaknesses and is ready to help us in our temptations and time of need (see also Hebrews 2:18). There is nothing of harshness or coldness when he deals with our souls; he is not strong in condemnation but short in encouragement. Leaders are to be like him. We have much more reason to be sympathetic and to bear with the weaknesses of others, and to seek to help them in time of temptation, because we are acutely aware of our own weaknesses and sinful falls. Having so many sins of our own we know that we are not fit to rebuke and deal with the sins and falls of others, and it is only because Christ has called us to this work, and because we long to keep our Christian friends from the sort of sins that have overtaken us, that we dare do it at all.

One further quality which needs to be mentioned is dedication to the task. It may be quite demanding to have managerial responsibility in a business, but it is not too difficult to act as a deacon or elder in a church so long as those responsibilities are thought of simply in terms of thoughtful and prayerful attendance at meetings, and carrying out certain tasks with reasonable diligence and faithfulness. However it is entirely different when leadership is thought of in terms of loving service and ministry to the church and its members. This requires a dedication to the task which can only come from the Lord and be sustained by him. To continue in selfless ministry in the midst of problems and difficulties, when people fail to appreciate you and do not recognise what you are trying to do or misunderstand, is a hard thing to do.

QUESTIONS FOR STUDY AND DISCUSSION

1. What do you think are the five most important qualities for leadership?

2. Is it right to aspire to leadership? What should such an aspiration lead to?

3. What aspects of leadership generally seen in secular life should not be brought into the church?

4. How can you lead by serving?

5. Case study: What does 1 Thessalonians 5:12-15 teach about the mutual relationships of leaders and members?

Leadership in practice

Does a stress on example and serving undermine the authority which leaders ought to have? How can they lead unless they exercise authority? In fact those who set an example which is followed are already leading. Those who are clearly devoted to serving all the members in love will be listened to, respected and their lead will be followed. Nevertheless it is important to consider the subject of authority.

AUTHORITY

Leaders do have authority. Jesus speaks of the 'one who rules' (Luke 22:26). In 1 Timothy 5:17, as we have seen already, the elders are to 'direct the affairs of the church', and 1 Thessalonians 5:12,13 says, 'Now we ask you, brothers, to respect those who work hard among you, who are over you in the Lord and who admonish you. Hold them in the highest regard in love because of their work.' Hebrews 13:17 says, 'Obey your leaders and submit to their authority. They keep watch over you as men who must give an account. Obey them so that their work will be a joy, not a burden, for that would be of no advantage to you.' (See also verse 7 of the same chapter.)

There is no need to say much more about authoritarianism. Part of the reason for the abuse of authority is that leaders sometimes have the impression that once being appointed they have a *personal* authority. Once a person's own feelings and sense of dignity get caught up in his responsibilities as a leader there is a great potential for broken relationships and discord. We live in days of general rebelliousness against authority and there is a danger of reacting to this in the churches, so that leaders try too hard to exercise authority. Leaders do have a spiritual authority but its nature must be understood by leaders and members.

The authority of the Word

The most important authority which leaders exercise is an authority which arises out of the Word of God. Leaders may be appointed because they have a sense of judgments and Christian prudence, but their supreme concern is to guide the flock according to God's Word. God's Word comes with God's authority. So on matters of principle which arise clearly out of the Bible there can be no compromise and leaders can take a clear stand. However, a note of caution needs to be sounded. It is not always quite so clear what is a plain Bible principle and what is simply one possible interpretation of what the Bible says. And even when the principle is clear, application of the principle is not always straightforward. Leaders must be honest and humble at this point. In the last analysis they must take their stand on what they are convinced together before the Lord is biblical principle, but before they reach that position they must study the Scriptures carefully and be able to explain why they take the view they do.

A matter of biblical principle is one thing; a matter of judgment is another. It can be personally upsetting if other leaders or the church reach a different judgment from the one you do, but there is no need to feel that your authority is being undermined, nor is there any call for a 'told you so' attitude if time demonstrates that you were correct. A realisation that authority arises out of the Word liberates us from feeling that we dare not disagree on matters of judgment, and helps us to put personal feelings where they belong.

Authority from calling

Authority also comes from a leader's calling. He is called by the Lord, and he is called through the church which appoints him to act as a leader. Leaders are then to be submitted to and obeyed, 'so that their work will be a joy, not a burden, for that would be no advantage to you' (Hebrews 13:17). There is no advantage to the church when there is on-going tension between leaders and members; there is no advantage when the leaders have no sense of joy in their work, because they are burdened by a constant sense of resistance to what they are trying to do. Some Christians seem to feel they have a mission to prevent leaders becoming overbearing and so they are always awkward and difficult and query practically everything their leaders suggest.

Authority from the nature of the work

Paul says of leaders, 'hold them in the highest regard in love because of their work' (1 Thessalonians 5:13). This work is not easy. It is highly responsible; leaders will have to give an account to *their* Lord and Leader (Hebrews 13:17). Christians are not like sheep in every respect. We can co-operate with our shepherds. We understand their work; we can make it easy for them, or hard, if we please. A few paragraphs ago a distinction was drawn between matters of judgment and matters of principle. Those appointed to leadership should be men of wisdom and discernment whose judgment can normally be trusted. Of course they are only flesh and blood and can be mistaken, but generally their judgment ought to be followed. In many cases there may be some difference of opinion within the church, and when there is it is the judgment of the leaders that should be heeded. That is why they are there. They are responsible before God; in fact in not a few cases members should feel it is a relief that they do not have to come to a final decision themselves, but that the decision, and hence the responsibility, lies on the shoulders of those appointed by the Lord.

Authority from a godly character

Authority also comes from character. The authority of a good leader is something you sense. There is something about his bearing, about his speech, about his attitude which breeds confidence in him. More than that; in the Christian this arises particularly from godliness and moral uprightness. When we say that leaders are desperately needed in these days in the churches, we do not simply mean we want more people to be appointed, we mean we desire to see the Lord giving to the churches those who are clearly men of moral and spiritual authority. It may be true that we get the sort of leaders we deserve; it is certainly true that some churches are not very likely to develop leaders with godly authority. This sort of authority grows out of all-round godliness; it is developed where Christians take their Christianity seriously; where there are real efforts, in reliance on the Holy Spirit, to live by the whole Word and to be increasingly conformed to Jesus Christ. We cannot say that leaders like this will always be recognised or have no opposition, but we can say that, in the main, such leaders are listened to and are able to exercise a godly authority within churches to their great advantage.

Shared authority

The authority of leaders is generally a shared authority. When leaders think of their authority in an individual way there is trouble as soon as there is any disagreement among them. If there is a shared leadership then there is a shared authority; authority inheres in the group, not in the individuals who make it up. If one leader dissents from the position of the rest then he must submit to the authority of the rest. In matters of principle a leader may feel it necessary to resign in order to keep his conscience clear, but there ought to be very few occasions like that in churches committed to Jesus Christ and his Word. There is something very important about this matter of shared authority. In any group of leaders there will be those with more experience than others; there will be those with more biblical and theological knowledge, those with more insight, those with a better knowledge of the members. These differences mean that all can bring different insights and contributions to the varied matters that have to be considered and decided. It is wisdom for leaders to recognise these differences and to defer to one another when it is appropriate to do so. Younger leaders will normally defer to the experience of the older; but when work amongst young people is concerned it will be wise for the older leaders to listen carefully to what younger colleagues have to say; and so on. When decisions have been reached, then they carry the shared authority of the whole leadership.

If leaders are given particular responsibilities, then there is an authority which goes with that responsibility. If a man is appointed to fulfil a particular function then he must be allowed to get on with it. The whole leadership will exercise a general oversight, but there is no point in sharing out responsibility if all the leadership still tries to discuss every decision. One of the ways in which unnecessary discussion and long meetings can be cut down is by making leaders responsible for different areas of the church's work. They then report briefly at meetings and only difficult issues need to be discussed by all the leaders together. Meetings which go on for several hours late into the evening are likely not only to tire leaders who may have a very full day before them next morning, but can also result in men speaking ill-advisedly out of tiredness or frustration. Instead of leaders' meetings being looked upon as joyful occasions when the Lord's work is being done, leaders get to dread them and this creates a cycle which can become progressively worse.

One more note about authority. In most independent churches the final authority rests with the church at a church meeting. There has to be a balance here. All matters which are vital for the whole church need to be brought to the church meeting. It is also right for members to have the right to raise any matter which they feel merits it. In many cases members are happy to be led by the leaders, and the ideal is to work for a situation in which this is the case. For this to come about, apart from the general confidence which the members need to feel in leaders, it is necessary for the leaders to be in close contact with the members and to listen to their concerns. At meetings leaders should explain clearly what has led them to bring a certain proposal to the church, and be ready to answer questions. Especially in matters which are likely to be contentious, if there are biblical principles involved these should be explained clearly, and everything should be done to carry the members by sound and spiritual reasoning. The leaders are to lead; the tail is not to wag the dog. However, they do not lead by *diktat* but by spiritual wisdom so that the members are glad to follow their lead.

THE WELFARE OF THE WHOLE

Leaders must be concerned for the welfare of the whole church. The spiritual welfare of all believers, however different from each other, and of the whole body as a living fellowship, is the responsibility of leaders. John Bunyan's *Pilgrim's Progress* is in two parts. The first part can be described as the pilgrimage of the individual soul and part two as the pilgrimage of the local church. This part is most interesting and instructive. The leader— the pastor?—of the pilgrims is called Great-heart. At one point the group of pilgrims is joined by Mr Feeble-mind, and Great-heart says to him, 'Come, Mr Feeble-mind, pray do you go along with us; I will be your conductor, and you shall fare as the rest.' But Feeble-mind replied, 'You are all lusty and strong, but I, as you see, am weak; I choose therefore rather to come behind, lest, by reason of my many infirmities, I should be both a burden to myself and to you.' 'But, brother,' said Great-heart, *'I have a commission to comfort the feeble-minded, and to support the weak. You must needs go along with us; we will wait for you; we will lend you our help; we will deny ourselves of some things, both opinionative and practical, for your sake; we will not enter into doubtful disputations before you; we will be made all things to you, rather than you shall be left behind.'* Here speaks a true leader of a church of pilgrims.

This, of course, is not easy. Earlier on in that part of Pilgrim's Progress Great-heart and Honest have a conversation about one called Mr Fearing. Honest said, 'He was a man that had the root of the matter in him: but he was one of the most troublesome pilgrims that ever I met with in all my days.' Great-heart. 'I was his guide from my Master's house to the gates of the celestial city.' Honest. 'Then you know him to be a troublesome one.' Great-heart. *'I did so; but I could very well bear it; for men of my calling are oftentimes intrusted with the conduct of such as he.'* These are words which leaders of churches could well commit to memory.

If leaders are going to promote the interests of the whole church, then they have to take care that they do not show favouritism, or even appear to do so. Leaders do not represent different factions in the church; they are not appointed to bring divisions that exist in the church into the leadership, and ensure that they are perpetuated. They are appointed to minister faithfully to the whole membership and work for the unity and harmony of the whole. It is not surprising if leaders have particular friends within the membership, but they must be careful about this. Christ had his inner core of disciples in Peter, James and John. We must not deny our humanity, which means that we may be closer to some than others. But this must never influence our decision-making or our ministry to the whole church.

Similarly some leaders may have particular responsibility for some aspect of the church's work or a particular interest or concern about some aspect, evangelism for example. Nevertheless they must not think of themselves as on the leadership to ensure that the aspect they are interested in is properly considered, they must be concerned about the whole body. From one point of view it is sometimes possible to see the church as a number of different interest groups, and sometimes there is an element of conflict between the aspirations of these groups. The leadership must be above all this. Their concern is to consider the whole church, all the members, every aspect of work and ministry, and to lead the whole church in ways that promote the welfare of all.

This does not mean that every member, or every part of the church's work, needs to be given the same time and attention. Some members, the

Mr Fearings and Mr Feeble-minds, for example—though also the Mr Prouds and Miss Haughtys—will always require more time and care. Those who shepherd the flock must be like the great Shepherd, 'He tends his flock like a shepherd: he gathers the lambs in his arms and carries them close to his heart; he gently leads those that have young' (Isaiah 40:11). Different aspects of the church's work will require more attention at different times.

In their concern for the whole church the leaders are also developing unity within the church. It is very easy for members to see only those aspects of the work which directly affect them. Sometimes members can seem oblivious to and even uninterested in aspects of the church's work. This naturally causes resentment on the part of those who work in those areas. In some prayer meetings much prayer is regularly offered for some activities and practically none for others. This means that the church has an unbalanced view of itself and this needs to be corrected. In actual fact the whole church should feel itself as involved and working together in all its different activities. 'From him (Christ) the whole body, joined and held together by every supporting ligament, grows and builds itself up in love, as each part does its work' (Ephesians 4:16).

DELEGATION AND COMMUNICATION

It is often easier to do something yourself than to delegate it to someone else. To start with you have to find someone who is willing to do it. Then you need to be sure he or she is going to carry out what you ask efficiently, thoroughly, and at the right time. You have to communicate what you want to have done. You might even feel you want to check up afterwards just to make sure that it has been done, as you wanted it done! In these circumstances it can seem easier to get on and do it yourself. For this reason many pastors and other leaders put burdens on themselves which are unnecessary and may distract from other more important matters. It also means that gifts and abilities which ought to be used by others are idle and not being developed. So delegation is important.

Delegation
Delegation is not the same as asking for volunteers. There is a place for this,

but in most cases it is best to consider the task which needs to be done or the position which needs to be filled, then to see who seems the most suited for it and approach that person. In many cases this will be done by the leaders considering together. Members may make known their willingness to be approached to help in the work of the church and in most cases this is an encouraging sign. Sometimes members with limited gifts are never asked to do anything and feel left out and frustrated as a result. Leaders with their eyes open will avoid such situations as far as possible. There is nearly always some task that can be given. On the one hand there is always plenty to be done; on the other it is important that as far as possible all the members play as full a part in the work of the church as possible.

Once some task has been delegated, unless the person concerned asks for help the right thing is to allow him or her to get on with the job. People naturally resent it if the impression is conveyed that the leaders don't have much confidence in them. It is right to ask how they are getting on from time to time, and to give encouragement and express appreciation when this is appropriate. If it becomes clear that a person is not up to the task that has been entrusted to them, it is best to have some alternative to offer. It is also important for there to be such a relationship between leaders and members that it is possible to talk over the situation and to discuss the question of gifts and suitability. Sometimes people take on responsibilities they are not suited for because they are afraid of revealing their misgivings, or because they know someone is needed, and they are glad to be able to talk things over frankly when it becomes clear they are struggling with the task.

Communication

What we have been discussing indicates the need for good communication within the church. Many problems arise simply because of a failure to communicate adequately. This may be so within a leadership. It may be there is not a proper liaison between elders and deacons. Sometimes just one or two leaders discuss a matter together and leave others out of it. There can be failures of communication between pastor and elders. These things cause resentment and suspicion among leaders. The issues themselves may not be particularly significant, but if some leaders feel they are being excluded they can take offence and personal relationships deteriorate within the leadership.

There needs to be good communication between the leaders of the church and the leaders of different departments within the church. Sometimes the problem is that one department—say, the youth work, or the women's meeting—becomes somewhat detached from the church as a whole, and from the oversight of the leaders. Leaders must guard against this. The church needs to be informed regularly about what is going on, and members must feel they are always free to talk to a leader about the work of the church.

Perhaps one word of warning needs to be added here. Leaders will necessarily have to discuss some matters that are confidential. This confidence must be absolute. Sometimes deeply personal problems have to be discussed, and people must be assured that their problems will never become public property in the church. In this connection it is extremely important for the wives of leaders to realise that their husbands may share with them things that must never be repeated to anyone else. In some cases I doubt whether leaders should share with their wives.

There are two other aspects to this. There are cases where a pastor or another individual leader will deal with a sensitive and private matter on his own. The whole leadership needs to be aware that they must not probe into such matters. They must have confidence to leave them with the leader concerned. On the other hand the leader must realise that he must watch out for situations which might compromise him. In such cases it will be better for him to have his wife or another leader present at the discussion, so he will need to get the consent of the person concerned for this.

There can easily be a tendency to sweep under the carpet matters which are public, and which need to be brought out into the light of day. This is a delicate matter, but it is possible to lay down some guidelines. If there is a truly repentant spirit, and the leaders, or a leader, are keeping a watchful eye on the situation it may not be necessary or wise for anything to be said publicly. If a member asks, it can be explained that the situation is being dealt with, without going into unnecessary detail. Church meetings, and individual members, do not need to be told everything about cases of moral failure. Church discipline needs to be exercised but the church meeting can never be like a court of law, where accusations and denials are weighed and judged. When information has to be given it must be known to be completely accurate.

EQUIPPING FOR MINISTRY

It is also a leadership responsibility to prepare those who are suitably gifted for the ministries they are capable of, and in some cases these will become leaders themselves. It is important that leaders, in the course of pastoral care, look out for gifts and abilities among the members. Included in this is the spotting of potential that has not yet had much opportunity for expressing itself. Some Christians are very eager to put themselves forward for service, in many cases because of a genuine love of the Lord and a desire to be useful in the work of the church. There are always others, however, who are less sure of themselves and their abilities, and who need help and encouragement in developing. Sometimes there are people who think too highly of their capabilities, or who wish to be involved in work for which they are not really suitable, or who simply would not fit in with others who are already doing the same work. Leaders have to be wise and try to help people into the most suitable service for them without discouraging them. Not a little tact and spiritual wisdom is needed for this.

Helping those who serve

In every church there will be people involved in a whole range of activities. In many cases they will have had no training at all for the work they are doing. Quite often they are left to get on with the work as best they can. Many have done sterling work and the Lord has graciously used them. However there are practical steps which can and should be taken to train and encourage. In addition to specific meetings or courses on subjects like Sunday School teaching, those who lead and work in specific activities within the church ought to be given basic advice in Christian leadership. A meeting twice a year or so of all those who work in the church—or a large area of the church's work like young peoples' work—to receive relevant ministry and for discussion of problems and prayer together is invaluable. Church leadership is not just a matter of keeping an eye on what happens and coming in when there are problems, or criticising those who may act unwisely, or preventing sectional leaders from doing something that is not approved of. It is more positive than that, and much more demanding. If it is done the rewards are great and the whole work will go forward much more harmoniously.

Preparing future leaders

There is also a responsibility to teach those whose gifts mean they may be able to take their place as leaders in future days. 2 Timothy 2:2 is well-known, 'And the things you have heard me say in the presence of many witnesses entrust to reliable men who will also be qualified to teach others.' How much can be done will depend on the number of leaders and how much else the church has in its programme, but there is a great variety of ways in which instruction and help can be given. At a simple level it is possible to suggest books and encourage young men with potential in reading them. If possible it is good for the pastor, or some other elder, to discuss what is being read. It is usually possible to have at least some seminars giving basic help on leading services, praying and reading in public, giving Bible studies, speaking or preaching. Theory and practice need to be mixed together. It is also necessary to teach biblical principles of leadership. This can also be done in various ways. For example, the book of Nehemiah is full of insight and help in this matter. On the other hand studies could be given on some of the crucial passages which have been referred to in this book.

A stage further is for a young man with promise and ability to be involved more completely in the work of the church or possibly some other Christian work. Members might be encouraged or financially supported to go on courses which would enable them to test their suitability and gain practical experience in some sphere of service. The practice of having a ministerial assistant who has just finished college or assistant pastor is extremely beneficial, both for the church and the man. Initially this can be a short-term commitment of, say, a year. It is possible to have placements of students from theological colleges for a certain period of time. The main stress in this book is on making such opportunities available for young men from within the church, under the supervision of the leaders. This is a responsibility which leaders should shoulder. It is not very valuable to have a pastoral assistant and then simply give him certain responsibilities and leave him to get on with them himself. While he will need opportunities to show initiative, he also needs the constructive fellowship and criticism which other leaders can give.

A further stage is theological and pastoral training. In the past such training often took place within local churches, and was undertaken by the pastor who might sometimes supervise the training of several men. This is not the place to debate the merits of church-based theological education against college training. In any case a great deal depends on circumstances. Only a very few churches are going to be able to provide theological education for pastors, though they do need to support those men who are preparing themselves for ministry.

In these days Bible exposition in services and midweek meetings needs to be at a fairly basic level, because many people do not have the biblical background which would be necessary for more thorough studies. It is also important that there is plenty of spiritual and practical application. As a result there is a great need for something more than this in the churches if sound teaching is going to be maintained and passed on to the next generation. For this reason it is good if there can be opportunity for more theological study available within the church for those who are prepared to spend sufficient time on it. This needn't be restricted to men preparing for the ministry; in fact it is a good thing if it is not, so that as many as possible can get a grounding in biblical teaching. Along with this we can mention teaching in the Christian approach to the social and ethical questions of the present day.

The ongoing training of leaders

Finally there is the ongoing training and development of the leaders themselves. The practice of pastors having study leave and sabbaticals for further study is increasingly recognised as valuable, and this could include pastors going on short courses either to refresh their knowledge or to study some particular area of doctrine more thoroughly. There are probably not many suitable courses available at present, but there are likely to be more short courses available in future. It is also valuable for other leaders to study particular aspects of teaching or pastoral work and more thought ought to be given to this. If leaders are going to function as a team then they need to develop their different gifts and develop skills which will contribute to the overall work of leadership.

QUESTIONS FOR STUDY AND DISCUSSION

1. In what ways do we see the authority of Jesus Christ in the New Testament?

2. What is the distinction between authority and authoritarianism?

3. What different ways of communicating information to church members can be used?

4. What training would be valuable in your church situation?

5. Case study: What does 1 Timothy 4:6-14 have to say to leaders?

A sense of direction

Leaders are to lead, but if they are going to do this they have to agree on the direction in which to go, and lead together. They have to reach agreement and continue in agreement, and it is not always easy to do either of these things. We shall explore some of the problems in this chapter.

POLICY DIFFERENCES

It is often quite easy for church leaders to deal with the day-to-day matters which come before them in their meetings, but it can be more difficult when it comes to broader areas of policy. Policy decisions concern matters like the standard of doctrine to which the church is committed; the way in which the worship is conducted; the overall commitment of the church to evangelism and the strategies adopted; relationships with other churches and extra-church bodies. They include guidelines for young people's work and the work of the Sunday School. We live in days when there have been major directional changes in many churches, and these have often taken place at the cost of dissension and sometimes division.

Reasons for differences

There can be various reasons why differences arise between leaders on matters like this. In some cases they arise because of different backgrounds and experience. Very often temperament is involved; some are naturally more cautious, others are eager to go forward and if necessary adopt new approaches. It helps if we can understand each other and remember that a blend of experience and temperament is usually a good thing. It is not generally so good if all the leaders are much the same in temperament and outlook. Agreement is easier, but there is not the same need to think through issues and consider them from different points of view, which is ultimately of great value.

One reason for differences is that different evaluations of the situation may be made. It is not easy to discern the real spiritual condition of a church, nor of the churches in general in an area, nor to discern what are suitable ways to reach unbelievers. Some churches have made sweeping changes and introduced all sorts of measures to try and reach unconverted people and have not been noticeably more successful than those who continued along much more well-trodden paths. The gift of spiritual wisdom, an understanding of the times and a knowledge of what God's people ought to do (see 1 Chronicles 12:32) are qualities which ought to be sought after, and leaders ought to do all they can, with God's help, to develop them.

Another reason for these broad areas of difference is that people understand the Scriptures differently. Part of the problem may be that the Bible is only known in a superficial way. Another difficulty is that many today say that the Scriptures have to be understood in their own culture, and as ours is different we cannot simply apply what the Bible says. Our culture, it is said, demands ways of doing things that are appropriate to it; for example we live in the television age therefore preaching is considered out of date and we are urged to adopt a far more visual approach to communicating the Gospel. While we must not act as if we lived in a past age, we must also ensure that the Bible is not sidelined, and its inspiration and authority as *God's* Word subtly undermined. Though given in temporal situations the Bible is God's Word and stands forever. It is sufficient to direct the worship and work of the churches right up until the time of the return of Jesus Christ. Humble, honest submission to Scripture, and prayerful and careful study of its pages will bring understanding and increasing agreement to leaders. When a matter is difficult leaders must not simply quote random texts at each other, the thing to do is to ask one or two to study the matter in depth and then set aside sufficient time for a proper discussion of what the Bible says.

Differences of opinion may also arise because leaders have different priorities. Some might think, for example, that before a church embarks on a new programme of outreach something ought to be done to strengthen the believers and unite them. Others might believe that a new commitment and involvement to evangelism would itself bring a new strength and unity to the church. There are often two ways of looking at things! In the last analysis differences of this nature are probably not of great significance. Of much greater importance is how they are handled and the readiness of leaders to learn from each other's point of view. In the example given, if attention is to be given first to the believers, the programme of evangelism to follow must not be lost sight of; or if the evangelism goes ahead it must not be thought that this is going to solve every other problem automatically. Once a decision has been taken leaders must go ahead *together.*

Assessing differences

It is also important to consider just how central an issue is when differences arise. Some changes could lead churches right out of evangelicalism altogether; some might certainly change the whole ethos if not doctrinal stance of the church. This may not be what anyone intends, but it is something that must be considered. The argument that a certain course of action is the thin edge of the wedge is a difficult one because any alteration can be seen as the beginning of some sort of a wedge. On the other hand a little yeast can work through the whole batch of dough (1 Corinthians 5:6), and many a hesitant step taken by a church has proved to put it on a slippery slope which has led inevitably to the bottom! But not all issues are of equal importance, not all policy decisions or changes in direction are going to lead to wholesale change. What is needed is spiritual, sober assessment by leaders who have developed spiritual wisdom, and who know where and how far they are going, and who can distinguish between big issues and matters of biblical principle, and those which are relatively minor. Possibly a minor difference of opinion can be managed, but differences on biblical principles have to be faced with earnest prayer for the mind of the Lord, honest study of the Bible and a recognition that all personal feelings and preferences must be subjected to the need to come to a godly agreement.

It is not surprising if from time to time individual leaders do not agree in every detail with their fellow leaders. It is much more serious when there is a real cleavage in a leadership, especially if this tends to show itself on a number of matters. All leaders ought to be deeply troubled when such a state begins to appear because this is the early symptom of a condition that may lead to bitter controversy and eventual division. There is no quick remedy to deal with it—though it is hoped that this book may prove helpful in such situations—but leaders must be alert to the serious consequences that could result and take all the steps they can to avoid them. Humiliation before the Lord, prayer with fasting, self-examination and confession to God, and in some cases to one another, will all have a place in putting the situation right.

Compromise and pragmatism are words which understandably have a bad reputation among Christians who desire to be faithful to the Lord and his Word. Nevertheless many churches have suffered because it is not recognised that there can be godly compromise and spiritual pragmatism. It is not at all wrong for leaders to come up with a policy which represents a compromise between different opinions if it is just a matter of opinion and personal preference. In such a case it is right to compromise. Pragmatism means adopting policies which are workable in the circumstances and with the personnel available. While great harm is done by spiritual compromise when it comes to the great truths and principles of God's Word, it is also true that equal harm is done by inflexibility and refusal to countenance anything being done in any other way than the way it has always has been done, or the way in which an individual feels it must be done.

PERSONALITY CLASHES

A great many differences of opinion go back to differences of temperament and personality. Most of us find we get on easily with some people, but find it much harder with others. Differences of upbringing, of background, of spiritual experience, of outlook, of wisdom, of knowledge of the Word of God, difficult experiences in the past, all these things can lead to personality clashes. It is quite often the case that personalities are involved in debates and arguments that *appear* to be about important doctrines or biblical principles. Underneath, however, there is personal animosity, misunderstandings have grown up, relationships have broken down, there is a lack of trust and understanding. It is sad to have to acknowledge it, but these things can be found within leaderships, and can at times seem almost insoluble.

There are some people who seem to feel that they are always right. They seem to believe that if their point of view is not respected and adopted then they are being rejected as persons and as Christians. There may be all sorts of reasons for them thinking like this, but it is very difficult for anyone to work with them. Probably they should not have been appointed as leaders in the first place, possibly they needed time to mature and grow as Christians, but in other respects they may be very gifted, and sometimes no-one realises what they are like until they are made leaders. Sometimes they feel it essential to try to get their own way whatever happens, and this usually causes a great deal of friction and distress.

In trying to prevent clashes of personality and the intrusion of personal feeling into the discussion of different policies and viewpoints, it is important for leaders to know themselves and to be very honest with themselves. The art of self-examination is rarely practised in these days, but self-examination in the light of the Bible and with prayer for the Holy Spirit's help is of great importance. It is also a good thing to try and put yourself into the other person's shoes. What do you honestly think they think about you? We all have self-defence mechanisms; we all know how to make excuses for ourselves. 'I shouldn't have spoken like that but…. I was tired; I wouldn't if he hadn't spoken first to me as he did; I'd been hassled all day; …' and so on. It is also a good thing for a leader to ask his wife to tell him frankly what his weaknesses and faults are; and perhaps to ask a good friend to help him in this respect as well. We all know prickly customers—undoubtedly Christians, good men in their way—and yet no-one dares speak to them about their faults and they are a constant source of irritation within a leadership or a church.

This leads us to realise that we must also try to understand each other. Leaders do sometimes speak testily because they are tired, have been provoked, or have been hassled all day. One of the problems is that church leaders usually have their meetings in the evening, often after a heavy day's work, when they are not fresh and when they would like to be able to relax for a while. The problem is compounded when they allow meetings to go on late into the evening when none of them are really fit to take wise and thoughtful decisions.

More than that it is essential to try and understand the temperaments and circumstances of fellow-leaders. We all have our personal weaknesses and blind-spots. There are occasions when everyone on the leadership knows what the reaction of one or two brothers is going to be. Mutual understanding and respect is very important, and also recognising the positive qualities of those who at times may seem to be rather negative in their general approach. At the same time we must avoid becoming manipulators of others, or knowing how to talk others round, or buttering them up. Mutual understanding is for the purpose of helping each other, and of being able to discuss matters taking into account differing approaches and being able to reach a common mind from the Scriptures.

As we have said, it is not always easy to distinguish between matters of principle and personal feelings and considerations which have got entwined with our principles. Nor is it always easy to distinguish between principle and personal preference. When we find ourselves getting angry and heated, when we find ourselves thinking more about the person whose view we object to than the view itself, when we feel wounded and sorry for ourselves because we don't think our views are being given proper consideration, then we should hear alarm bells ringing. Even if what we think is right, our attitude is almost certainly wrong. Unfortunately one of the reasons why biblical principles are sometimes over-ridden in churches is because those who argue for them display attitudes which do not seem to reflect Christian love and a desire for God's glory. People reason that if the attitude is wrong probably the principle being put forward is mistaken as well.

CHANGES AFTER APPOINTMENT

This problem has already been referred to earlier, but it needs to be considered more thoroughly. Leaders do alter in their opinions and change their views with time and this can sometimes lead to a great deal of difficulty and tension. Perhaps the first thing to acknowledge is that this should not just be viewed in a negative way. It is because Christians mature, it is because the Lord gradually knocks off the rough edges, it is because people's sympathies enlarge and they see things from a broader perspective, that mutual understanding grows and develops and leaders become welded together as a team. If none of us ever grew out of the impetuousness of youth; if we all stopped learning once we had reached—say—twenty-five, then the churches would be in a sorry state!

Always growing

Growth and development are to mark the lives of Christians. We might well take note of the words of Paul in his letter to the Philippians, 'Brothers, I do not consider myself yet to have taken hold of it. But one thing I do: Forgetting what is behind and straining towards what is ahead, I press on towards the goal to win the prize for which God has called me heavenwards in Christ Jesus. All of us who are mature should take such a view of things. And if on some point you think differently, that too God will make clear to you. Only let us live up to what we have already attained. Join with others in following my example, brothers, and take note of those who live according to the pattern we gave you' (3:13-17).

Paul expects all whom he describes as 'mature' to take the same view and to be committed to pressing forward. Mature Christians recognise how immature they still are and how much more there is still to learn! Then, too, Paul expects God to bring agreement amongst his people where they differ. As they press forward so they will gradually come closer together because they are aiming at the same mark, they are going to the same destination. He urges his readers to live up to their attainments. There is always the danger of slipping back or of acting inconsistently. Paul urges the Philippians to use their present knowledge and experience as the foundation on which they build for the next stage in their progress.

Though Paul uses himself as an example and so focuses on himself as an individual the application is in terms of the members of the church growing together. We tend in these days to think of Christian growth as an individual thing, but this is a mistake. The whole church should be growing together; all who are mature will be pressing forward; we are to join with others in following Paul's example. This means that leaders should be growing together, too: in developing the qualities needed to fulfil their responsibilities, in acting together in the Lord's work, in mutual understanding and wisdom, and in care for the people. In this way they become more able to function as a body of leaders.

Many temptations

Leaders are also subject to all the temptations that are common to Christians. It is doubtless true that the devil will attack leaders more frequently and in more subtle ways than he does other Christians. If he can introduce dissension, or worldly thinking and unspiritual considerations into the leadership he is well on the way to harming the whole church. Just as other Christians, leaders go through cycles in their spiritual experience. They have their times of special difficulty; they go through barren periods when the Lord's presence is not as near and real as it used to be; they struggle in their times of devotion and prayer. Leaders must realise that these things are possibilities for them, and that they can expect special attacks from the devil. These attacks may, I think, also be in terms of illness, extra responsibilities being piled on at work, problems in the home or with relatives. When a leadership seems to be functioning well and beginning to act as it should in leading God's people forward, be ready for these things.

This means, too, that leaders should be sensitive to each other and the difficulties that others may have. There should especially be a loving sensitivity to spiritual difficulties and prayer for one another.

If a leader gets too burdened with many different responsibilities, for example if he moves to a new job or his wife becomes ill, it may be right for him to be given a period of leave from leadership. It is often better to do this rather than for the leader concerned to resign from his position, especially if everything seems to point in the direction of this being a temporary matter. This will partly depend on how leadership arrangements are made in a particular church. Unfortunately many churches are very inflexible and leaders have to resign or stand down at the next election and then be voted in again at an annual meeting—perhaps in three years time! All this does is harm the church and make it appear that it does not understand the pressures people may be under nor know how to deal with its leaders in caring and sensitive ways.

Although the ideal would seem to be for Christians to grow steadily and for their views to change and mature gradually over time, it seldom happens quite like this. When we begin to see some truth, or aspect of truth, we had not realised before, we often embrace it enthusiastically and swing perhaps from one extreme to another. Immediately we become zealots in the cause of getting everyone to see as we now see, and changing the church as quickly as possible to take on board what we believe to be so vital. This is very human, but hardly helpful within the leadership! One of the evidences of real growth is that we do not react like this. We become aware of our tendency to go to extremes and we take care to integrate our new insight with what we know already to be biblical truth. Some people are always discovering something new, and when they do, it fills the whole of their horizon for a while until it is displaced by something else. Unless they show some evidence of change towards a more balanced position it is probable they are not suited for leadership, even though they may have some gifts—which they may well be anxious to exercise! Gifts alone are never enough; godliness and a biblical balance and sense of proportion are much more important.

Personal integrity

Leaders must be men of integrity. They will know what the standpoint of the church is on all important doctrinal matters. If they begin to change their views then they have a responsibility to make this clear. They must be honest in discussion, and honest in listening to others. It is no good putting down the concerns of others simply to prejudice or misunderstanding. Honest prayerful discussion will lead to prejudices and misunderstandings being seen for what they are, but to start off assuming that those who disagree with you are guilty of one or the other is foolish and sinful. Younger men must respect the experience of older men. Older leaders are not always right, but in matters of judgment and when it comes to seeing the implications of a change of doctrinal view they ought to be. If they have not learned the lessons that only experience can teach, then there is no-one else around who has learned them either.

One other matter can be considered at this point. This is the difficult area of the balance between matters of personal conscience and corporate responsibility. Generally speaking we lay the emphasis on individual conscience. From one point of view nothing is more important than to keep a clear conscience before God. Yet not everything is a matter of the individual conscience. A leadership has to act together. It has to take decisions which will not always have one hundred per cent agreement of all the leaders. Corporate responsibility means that in matters which are not essential, which do not violate the conscience before God, leaders agree a certain course of action together, and then together stick to it. Of course if necessary they can review it together, and sometimes change their minds; leaders are not infallible after all. Some do not seem to understand that there has to be corporate responsibility and the submission of personal conscience in the interests of the good of the whole. This is a vital point; if everything is made a matter of personal conscience it becomes impossible to have churches at all.

DECISION-MAKING

As leadership decisions are made in leadership meetings, the way in which these are conducted is very important. Some leaders seem to find it very hard to reach decisions which keep getting deferred to another meeting. Some meetings seem to go round in circles, and sometimes circle on very late. Other meetings cause frustration, at least to some of the leaders, because they appear to be cut and dried. The pastor, or one or two leaders, seem to have their own agenda which is pushed through every time. There is no proper discussion and those who don't agree are too weak to raise objections or they know that if they do it will be so unpleasant that it is better to keep quiet. How should leadership meetings be conducted?

A spiritual approach

There is obviously no one way, certainly not one laid down in Scripture, but there are certain aspects which can be discussed. Most important of all is that all meetings are conducted in a spiritual atmosphere, with prayer that is not merely perfunctory, with submission to the Word of God and a desire to do what will glorify Christ. Christ is the chief shepherd and under-shepherds have no right to any plans or designs of their own; everything must be done for him. It is easy enough to agree to this, but it is another thing to have the heart submissive to Christ and to be ready to put his glory and the interests of his kingdom first. Sometimes leaders ought to stop their discussions to pray. If the atmosphere gets very tense it may be right to adjourn the meeting, realising that this is an admission of serious failure that needs to be repented of and that the next meeting must be approached with suitably chastened spirits. It is not at all inappropriate for leaders to be reminded of the words of Ephesians 4:31,32: 'Get rid of all bitterness, rage and anger, brawling and slander, along with every form of malice. Be kind and compassionate to one another, forgiving each other, just as in Christ God forgave you.'

Wise chairmanship

Any meeting to make decisions needs a chairman. Sometimes his task is not very onerous, but the greater the number of participants the more need there is for good chairmanship. This is especially true if the subject is a difficult and contentious one. In many cases the pastor is expected to take the chair; quite often *he* expects to take the chair! This may be the best in many instances, but it should not be thought to be an invariable rule. If pastors today are usually thought of as preachers and teachers of the word it is not obvious that the gifts needed for such ministry will suit them for chairmanship. In some cases the chairmanship may rotate amongst the leaders; this may work well in some cases, but generally there will be some leaders who are not very suitable and who probably would much prefer not to have to take their turn. A good chairman will be someone who has prepared beforehand, as far as possible; who keeps the discussion moving, who brings it back from digressions, and ensures that everyone who wants to say something has an opportunity to do so. He keeps his eye open to see if anyone seems unhappy with the direction things are going, and he is good at summing up the general consensus. A good chairman is not simply someone who knows how to manipulate a meeting so that it always ends up deciding the way he wanted from the beginning. A chairman must have a certain detachment while he is chairing. This is difficult when he may have a clear conviction about what he believes is the Lord's will. A good chairman is marked by spiritual wisdom.

Indecision

Some leaders' meetings fail because the leaders are not decisive enough. Whilst the work of a church ought not to be compared to that of a business, if businesses dillied and dallied in the way some leaderships do they would soon be in financial difficulties and end up bankrupt. It is dishonouring to the Lord if his work is conducted in a way that no person in secular life would tolerate for a moment. Leaders need to come together with the aim of deciding those matters that need deciding. Leaders need to realise that every time a decision is put off it is in fact a decision to do nothing, a decision to dither. If a matter is complex and needs thinking, and then talking, through, this should be recognised at the beginning and time set aside to deal with it, perhaps at a special meeting just for that matter. The more decisions are deferred the more the agenda gets clogged with items that keep returning, causing leaders coming to meetings to feel overwhelmed even before they have started.

Many leaders' meetings are quite informal and perhaps this is how they should be. At the same time it is very valuable for all the leaders to be provided with succinct minutes, especially with regard to ongoing matters. Minutes do not need to be long; just the decisions, or the main points raised if the matter is to be taken up again. It helps if there is an agenda which is given out beforehand; or at least for leaders to know if any particularly important matter is going to come before a meeting. Leaders need to be able to pray and think over the items that will be dealt with at the meeting. This is not to suggest that nothing can be brought to the meeting by a leader at the time, only that if possible it is a good thing to be able to prepare.

Speaking and listening

At meetings there should be opportunity for leaders to express their opinions frankly. Some people, of course, are too frank and put forward their views with a certain amount of belligerence. Sometimes this is because they have to screw themselves up to do it at all. If the atmosphere is right and other leaders are understanding this may correct itself in time. Younger men are quite likely to fall into this category, and some allowance can be made for them in this respect. No-one likes to be either patronised or ignored, and both of these attitudes should be avoided. It is important for leaders to listen to each other. The impression is sometimes given that one leader is not listening to another, simply waiting for an opportunity to make his own voice heard. Leaders should be listeners who can pick up feelings and attitudes which underlie what is being said. This quotation, from a book on quite a different subject, is relevant not just to leaders meetings but to the work of leadership in general: 'There is no better way of assuring a person that you are a perceptive listener than when you identify the feeling that lies underneath the words. To spotlight the feeling and label it is the quickest way to making a person feel understood. And when a person feels understood, he or she becomes less defensive and more co-operative' (Selwyn Hughes, *Marriage as God Intended,* Kingsway; p.60.).

The aim of any committee meeting is to use the strengths of all the committee members. Some leaders will have experience in one area, others in another. Everyone ought to feel that they can contribute; everyone ought to be made to feel that if they withhold their contribution the result will be the poorer for them all. All the leaders are together in the providence of God. This doesn't mean that all will continue as leaders in the longer term, in some cases some who prove to be unsuitable become leaders for a while, often men who have recognised their own limitations have held the fort and done a splendid job until the Lord has brought in others to take over from them. But if hearts and attitudes are right before the Lord, he will enable leaders to function together while they are together, and to serve him in the present situation.

TENSIONS IN THE CHURCH

In most churches there will be certain tensions, though they may not be very great. Christians think differently, and there are likely to be those who are more progressively minded, those who are more cautious, those who are more traditional and those who want to get on with things. Similarly there may be those who lean more in one direction doctrinally and others more in another. All this is more or less inevitable and it is not at all surprising if these tensions are reflected within the leadership. It may well be a good thing if they are. Tensions that are recognised and that are not too great may prove to be creative and helpful. It is not a good thing, for example, if the church's leaders are all much the same in temperament; a leadership of all extroverts or all introverts would not be very helpful. At the same time tensions are not always good. Some tensions arise because some people are always pulling in a particular direction; they are always trying to get the church more to their way of thinking and doing things. Leaders must learn to rise above this. As we have seen, they must always have a concern for the whole church.

Factionalism

In some cases tensions can result in factions, that is groups of people with their own agenda. Sometimes leaders appear to see themselves as representatives of a faction. Sometimes the members of the faction see the leader in the same way; 'At least we've got so-and-so on the leadership now'! However understandable this may be, and though sometimes one faction may in fact be a faithful remnant, this situation is extremely unhealthy. The main answer to it seems to be for leaders to get back to the Scriptures and see what their responsibilities are. They are not called to represent different power groups in the church; they have positive functions to which they are called by Christ himself, and they had better get down to doing what he has given them to do. Sometimes the situation is even more complex because a faction may be made up largely of people of the same family. Families can be the blessing or the bane of churches! As in so many cases what has potential for great good has potential for harm also. The church must learn to see itself more as one spiritual family, the 'family of believers' (Galatians 6:10), than as a loose grouping of natural families with strong natural ties and loyalties. It is worth noting that when the mother and brothers of Jesus came, wanting to speak with him, 'he replied... "Who is my mother, and who are my brothers?" Pointing to his disciples, he said, "Here are my mother and my brothers. For whoever does the will of my Father in heaven is my mother and sister and brother"' (Matthew 12:48-50). Not all church members put those who do the will of the Father before natural family loyalties. Jesus also said, 'Anyone who loves his father or mother more than me is not worthy of me; anyone who loves his son or daughter more than me is not worthy of me' (Matthew 10:37). It is sobering to apply these words in the context of the church of Jesus Christ; how can we harm or divide the body of Christ in the interests of our own relatives?

Although it can be difficult to have on the leadership those who in some sense represent tensions or factions in the church, it is worse when there is a faction in the church which is disaffected with the leadership. Sometimes almost the whole church can be in that position. This usually happens where the leadership keeps strict control of church affairs, tends to be rather secretive and allows very little discussion of church matters in church meetings. It expects that the membership will simply ratify whatever is put to it. Such widespread disaffection cannot happen if the leaders are doing their job properly and ensuring adequate pastoral care of the congregation. It is rather different if there is just a group who seem always to be against whatever the leaders say. Sometimes this will be because there is a trouble-maker, or trouble-makers, among them. Unfortunately there are people within churches, they may be real Christians too, who for a variety of reasons cause a great deal of trouble. If it is some personality disorder, or temperamental problem, and the members recognise that this is the case there is not likely to be much real damage done in the church, even though it takes time and grace to help those who are like this. When a group is concerned the leaders will have to evaluate the situation carefully. It may prove to be the case that the differences are so great, or grow so great, that in the end the group leaves. This is always very sad, even though in some circumstances it may be the only thing that can be done. Because circum-stances and causes of difference can be so diverse it is not possible to try to give any guidance about what steps can be taken. But everything reasonable must be done to prevent a group from becoming an insulated faction, and this includes listening carefully to their concerns and being as flexible as principle will allow, though recognising that one group must not be allowed to influence the church against the general will.

Change

Every church has to change; in fact most churches are gradually changing all the time. Change can be good or bad, but times come when fairly major changes need to be made. There may be a whole variety of reasons for this—though at the time not everyone may realise it. It is often difficult to manage change, and many churches have suffered greatly when they have tried to change. A great deal of the problem is one of perception. There are those who think that in a changing world, the church should be a haven of stability if not predictability. There is some truth in this, of course, which is ignored at our peril. Part of the problem is that we do not realise how much the churches have changed over the years. None of us now worships exactly as the Puritans did, neither would it be possible or desirable to try to do so. We live in a changing world. Language changes, faster now than ever before. Musical tastes change; standards of comfort change. In America the Pilgrims resisted for years the introduction of heating into their meeting-houses, but few want church buildings like that today. The important thing is for leaders to be agreed themselves about changes; and for them to be able to explain clearly to the church what the changes involve and why they ought to take place. Small changes gradually introduced, which are also easy to reverse if it proves necessary to do so, are much better than delaying change so that major changes have to take place all at once. It is also important to conserve our heritage and to ensure that worship expresses the old truths in a contemporary way.

Biblical priorities

In many churches the role of leaders seems to include keeping people 'happy'. The basic principle seems to be to ensure that nobody rocks the boat. Everything revolves around the idea of making sure that no-one is going to be too unhappy with what is going on. This is understandable, but it is far from satisfactory. It is likely that the application of biblical principles will make a few decidedly unhappy. While there must always be sensitivity to how people think and feel, this cannot be the final arbiter for church life. Leaders must teach from the Bible and ensure that the worship and work of the church conforms to biblical principles. For example, worship must be reverent as well as intelligible; it must be simple and spiritual. It must be directed primarily to God; worship is for his glory not our entertainment. Or consider evangelism. The message must not be compromised by the method. Short cuts to get people to make an easy commitment have to be avoided. It is one thing to make the message of the gospel relevant to people today, it is quite another to adapt it to the desires and needs which people think they have.

There are certain essentials for welding a church into a unity and keeping it together. At the centre of church life there has to be a full-orbed ministry of the Word of God. The great truths of the gospel need to be often brought before the people, but in their biblical proportion and expounded from the Scriptures. The souls of God's people need to be fed and nourished; nothing can compensate for the lack of this, whereas even if there are many other weaknesses they can be borne with if the spiritual life is being truly nurtured. Leaders must be prayerful themselves in their meetings and personally, and ensure that prayer is also central to the life of the church, so that everything begins with prayer and continues with prayer. Too many churches pay lip service to the importance of prayer. The members of the church need to be active in the work of the church. Where leaders do practically everything, and are not keen on delegating anything to anyone else, instead of being busy and devoting themselves to their responsibilities the members feel slighted, unfulfilled, and they have plenty of time to think, and perhaps talk, critically about the leaders! A church needs also to have a commitment to evangelism. Where these four elements are found; Bible ministry, prayer, an active membership and evangelistic outreach it is likely that tensions will be kept to a minimum and everyone will worship and work together for the glory of Christ.

KNOWING EACH OTHER AND GROWING TOGETHER

Leaders have got to work together and take decisions together. It is important for them, then, to take steps to know and understand each other. This is necessarily something that comes over time, but there are ways of ensuring the process takes place. It is surprising how little some church members really know of each other even after years in the same church. When leaders understand each other then they have confidence in each other and are able to help each other.

Part of the difficulty is that leaders meetings have full agendas of items which have to be considered. The atmosphere is not usually relaxed and there isn't time to pay much attention to relationships. Very often, too, church leaders are very busy men in their own employment, as well as being engaged in many activities of the church. Not only in spite of these things, even more because of them, it is good if leaders can spend time with each other more informally than at their regular meetings. There are various ways of doing this.

At the simplest level leaders could have a meal together before their meeting, or have a breakfast together on a Saturday morning which either leads into a regular meeting—though perhaps on an unusual day, or a time of prayer and/or discussion of some specific matter which needs time by itself. Some leaders have 'retreats' when they go away for a day, or spend Friday evening and Saturday together. It is not a good thing for the whole leadership to be away over the Lord's Day, though exceptional circumstances might make it necessary. On such occasions it is usually possible for the leaders to have a walk together, to talk together about their families and work, and for them to get to understand each other as persons and Christians.

Very often one or two leaders will already be close friends. This has potential for good, but also for harm. That is not wrong in itself; human friendship is commended in Scripture (Proverbs 18:24) and we should expect it in the church. However, if it means that some leaders never mix much or talk much then it becomes dangerous. When it leads to friends ganging up with their own agenda it can be extremely divisive. Moreover real friendship can survive disagreements; there is no need for friends to think they always have to agree with one another or back each other up.

Leaders need to grow together spiritually, also. In some cases quite the opposite happens. Because of differences of opinion expressed in meetings men can grow apart. Apart from prayer at every leaders' meeting it is also good for leaders to meet together just to pray, or perhaps for Bible study and prayer. On some occasions a biblical or practical theme could be opened up and discussed. In fact leadership meetings ought to be much more about these things than they usually are. Part of the problem of the days in which we live is that churches are faced with new teachings and practices, new styles of worship, new proposals for evangelism, but there has never been any time for leaders to think these through biblically and theologically. Leaders have had to react quickly to propositions and pressure without having ever had the opportunity to study the Word of God together. Many leaders don't get much time to read books and often they have not really been competent to handle the matters that have arisen. Leaderships need to remedy this as much as they can.

When new leaders are appointed the existing leadership should make it as easy as possible for them to settle in quickly. Younger men often feel a bit out of their depth for a while. It is not a bad idea for the existing leaders to try and put themselves into the position of a new leader coming to his first meeting. Would his first impression be one of disappointment? Would he feel that the atmosphere was too frivolous, or too tense? Would he feel matters were being attended to responsibly and spiritually? Older men can sometimes resent younger men coming on to the leadership; younger men can sometimes be too cocky, endowed with all the tact of a new broom. A leadership which has been together for a long time can become a coterie that resents the thought of anyone else coming and 'spoiling the fellowship' they have. Love, forethought, a little understanding, can make all the difference and ensure that adding to the leadership enhances its usefulness and does not introduce ill-feeling or tension.

QUESTIONS FOR STUDY AND DISCUSSION

1. How can a person distinguish between conviction and personal preference or prejudice?

2. What makes a good chairman?

3. What practical steps can leaders take to develop good relationships with each other?

4. Should leaders have aims and goals for the church? If so, what should these be?

5. Case study: What principles for leadership and initiating new work are provided by Acts 13:1-5?

Part IV

Keeping in tune

The final section of this book is concerned with watching out for problems and difficulties, restoring relationships after they have become strained or broken down and going forward harmoniously in the church and keeping it like that. It is much easier to do the first and last of these things. Yet in many situations it is restoration which is needed. In her recent biography of William Grimshaw, Faith Cook records this about him: 'Confronted by believers who refused to be reconciled to one another, Grimshaw had been known to fall on his knees and beg them with many tears to love each other in the bonds of the gospel. Going even further, Mrs Joseph Jones records that on one occasion, when he was trying to conciliate two querulous believers, she heard him say, "I beg you upon my knees: I will put my head under your feet, if you will but love one another." His own passionate concern for unity between them had so great an effect both on them and others present at the time, that "all in the house were melted down in tears and perfectly reconciled."' (Faith Cook, *William Grimshaw of Haworth*, Banner of Truth; p.230/1).

Perhaps we do not value love and unity as Grimshaw did, nor are our hearts as passionately concerned to promote these things as his was. His is the attitude we need to see grow in our hearts as we consider what the Bible says and as the Holy Spirit impresses its truth upon us. We need to value peace in the churches, watch out for all those things which tend to undermine or harm it, and seek to be peacemakers among God's people. It is striking that our Lord should say, 'Blessed are the peacemakers, for they will be called sons of God' (Matthew 5:9). It is peacemakers who are like their Father, and who are carrying out that work which especially shows them to be his sons.

Problem areas

This chapter tries to examine the various areas of church life and leadership responsibility in which problems are particularly likely to arise. Because we have a subtle enemy, and are still troubled with indwelling sin, problems can occur in any area of the life of a church. Yet some areas have proved to have particular difficulties and we shall try to cover these. It is one thing to identify a problem, it is another to be able to solve it. Problems occur in the particular circumstances of a church with its own personnel. There are, therefore, no answers which cover every circumstance, there are only suggestions and pointers which churches and leaders can use if they find them appropriate and helpful. Often identifying the problem goes a long way to finding its solution.

STRUCTURE

Structure refers to the way the church is organised and the way in which church matters are dealt with. Some churches have a very rigid structure. They have a very clear view of the way in which a church ought to be governed; let us say, pastor, elders, deacons. They have detailed rules about the functions and appointment of these leaders, the conduct of church meetings, the appointment of other workers, the discipline and restoration of those who sin, and every other matter which has arisen in the life of the church has been brought under the scope of the church rules.

Other churches appear to have very little structure at all, or one which is variable. They get by on an *ad hoc* basis. Church meetings are conducted in the way which suits the incumbent pastor, or perhaps the church secretary if there is no pastor. They may tend to justify the way they do things by saying they don't want to be tied down by rules and regulations, rather they want to make room for the liberty of the Spirit. Churches of both types may actually function quite well, with a fair degree of harmony. Yet it is surely clear that both of these extremes open the way for problems.

Structured but flexible

The church which seems to have everything cut and dried may easily end up doing things in a mechanical way. Rules can sometimes prevent wise flexibility and adaptability to changing circumstances. Of course rules can be changed, but it takes time to do so, and it is easy for a church to get into the habit of doing things in a certain way. If a rule often needs to be changed this suggests it is not wise to have it at all or that it is too tightly drawn. More important, perhaps, than these considerations is the fact that the atmosphere of the church can become rule oriented. Many rules about the appointment of leaders and the conduct of church meetings have no direct biblical warrant. There is nothing in the Bible to suggest that a deacon needs to get 75% of a vote in a church meeting in order to be appointed, for example. Many rules adopted by churches are wise; there has to be some way of deciding what support from the church is needed before a deacon can be appointed. A basic minimum of rules and a readiness to consider questions in the light of circumstances seems the best approach.

On the other hand churches with virtually no structure at all are in great danger from a whole range of people, from the immature to the strong-minded, if they gain influence in the church. There needs to be some positions of responsibility and some agreed way of doing things. One of the reasons for a type of continuous anarchy in a church is because the members cannot agree on government or how things should be done. It is simply foolish to allow a situation like that to go on. It should be possible to come to some basic positions unless some members are merely being obstructive. In that case the majority must take decisions, and with as much grace and understanding as possible, put in place a framework for church life and decision-making.

Structured but suited to the church's circumstances

In thinking about a church structure circumstances need to be taken into account. If it's a small church, with no elders and few deacons, there is no great value in setting out distinctions between elders and deacons, with division of functions and methods of appointment. Structures need to be suitable for the size and state of the church, the people who are suitable for leadership and the type of ministry which is available. As a church grows so structures can be adapted for a different situation and different needs. If a church shrinks there is no sense in trying to cling on to ways of doing things which belonged to the past, when simplifying things would meet the immediate need much better.

Some will probably feel that this is a very pragmatic approach. Is there not a biblical pattern to which all churches ought to conform? Certainly all churches must regulate their affairs by the Word of God, but it is clear that those who are equally committed to the full authority of Scripture do not and are never likely to agree in detail on all aspects of church government and life. We have already seen examples where differences of opinion occur. That there is a basic pattern in Scripture is unquestionable, but it can be applied in a variety of ways. I would argue that this flexibility is itself scriptural and intended by the Lord. Churches come in many shapes and sizes, from the many thousand strong church of Jerusalem in Acts to the small independent churches of Great Britain today. They are planted and grow in many different cultures, rightly taking their flavour from that culture so that the reformed churches of Scotland have historically differed from the reformed churches of Wales, which differ again from the reformed churches of England. They are made up of Christians whose background and upbringing differs considerably, those with a Jewish background and those with a Gentile background; those who have a long Christian heritage, those who are first-generation Christians with pagan backgrounds. Some have many men with leadership potential among them, others have few. It is not surprising if there are variations in detail among churches, nor does it matter at all. The important thing is that they function as churches should, that they grow and develop and are always reforming themselves according to the Word of God.

A living relationship to Christ

The basic starting-point is that Jesus Christ is the head of the church. Some give the impression that they understand 'head' in this connection as if it were short for 'headmaster', but this is quite the wrong picture. Christ is head of the church as the head is related to the body, (1 Corinthians 12:27; Ephesians 1:22,23; 4:15,16; 5:23,24; Colossians 1:18). The emphasis is not on Christ as lawgiver but on the living, spiritual relationship which exists between him and the churches. Submission to Christ as head is not simply a matter of outward obedience, it is the submission of heart and life in every respect to the One who is the Saviour of the body (Ephesians 5:23), who gave himself up for the church in order to make her holy and present her to himself as a perfect bride (Ephesians 5:25-27). This includes obedience to the commands and conformity to the instructions of Scripture, but it is much more than that and cannot be reduced to it. This has to be stressed because it is so fundamental. The Reformation was not about replacing aesthetic worship with ascetic worship, or replacing, in Milton's words, 'old priest' by 'new presbyter', it was about a spiritual revolution which brought the gospel, faith, grace, the Bible and Christ himself to the very centre of Christianity. Everything about real Christianity throbs with the vitality of a living relationship to Jesus Christ. The pattern of church life is important, but if the pattern is put before the Person, rather than being received from him, everything is lost.

MODELS OF LEADERSHIP

Many churches have suffered because the models of leadership they have followed have been taken from the world of business rather than from the Bible. One of the features of the past fifteen years or so has been the introduction of leadership courses for pastors and church workers which have been based on experience in the secular realm. Men with drive and initiative who have done well in business often become leaders in their own churches and tend to bring their own ideas of leadership from their experience at work. This is not necessarily bad; there are different ideas concerning leadership in business, and some of them have useful insights, but it is very important for churches and leaders and potential leaders to take their standards from Scripture. When men try to be directors or executives in the church the work is bound to suffer.

Variation of leadership styles

We also need to remember that everyone is different, so there is bound to be a variation of leadership styles. This is particularly noticeable with pastors. Some men are very much individuals and there is no point in trying to press their individuality into a mould that suppresses them so much that they cannot be themselves. At the same time they must be aware that they have to co-operate with others and they must not ride roughshod over the convictions and sensitivities of others. For example, there would have been no point in trying to get the 19th-century preacher C.H Spurgeon to work in a system where the parity of elders was practised. After looking over a great deal of the work of the Metropolitan Tabernacle someone reported this fascinating interchange: "'Mr Spurgeon,' I could not help saying, "you are a regular Pope!' 'Yes,' he replied, 'though without claiming infallibility. This is indeed a democracy, with a large infusion of constitutional monarchy in it.'" (Arnold Dallimore, *Spurgeon*, Banner of Truth Trust, p.159). Not everyone is like Spurgeon, and the problem is there are always those who try to copy well-known ministers without having the same gifts that they had. Other men find it easier to operate where there is a shared leadership. They need the support of fellow leaders, both in coming to decisions and in bearing the burden of problems and difficulties.

Highly individualistic and motivated men can often be a problem in a church. The entrepreneurial type and the free spirit find it difficult to work within the framework of a corporate leadership and church life. In the New Testament there seem to have been many more who were engaged in itinerant ministry than is generally the case today. The demise of the evangelist has been partly responsible for this. We need to make room in our thinking and practice for men of vision and drive to spearhead Gospel work in new areas, or to visit an area for a limited period in order to engage in evangelistic work. We have over-emphasised the local church as the *sphere* of ministry just as we have wrongly given the impression that the pastoral ministry is the only valid calling in these days. This is not suggesting that evangelists and gospel-preachers should have no connection with any local church; they should belong to one and recognise its leadership, so that their work comes under the general supervision of its leaders. They should also, as far as possible, work with and through local churches in their evangelism. But they should be set *free* to use their gifts and individuality for the Lord.

There are those whose gifts and bent is more towards organisation and management. Such gifts have their place, but they can do a great deal of harm in stifling the gifts of others in the church, and making themselves indispensable to everything that goes on. In the early 19th century there was a prominent Methodist called Jabez Bunting of whom it was said, 'The Methodist Conference was buttoned up like a pair of trousers, and they were worn by Jabez Bunting'! Churches (and Conferences and denominations!) can flourish under the leadership of such people. The trouble usually comes after they leave and it is found impossible to find anyone else who really slots into the position that they have made for themselves. It is usually not until it is almost too late that it is realised that the best thing is to reorganise according to the personnel and gift available rather than trying to follow the precedent set by the great man.

Group influence

At the opposite end of styles of leadership there is what can be called the cabalistic. The word 'cabal' means a clique; a group of five ministers who served under Charles II had initials which could be made to form this word. Sometimes a whole leadership can be like this, or at other times it is a group within the leadership. Such a group tends to be secretive, no-one really knows what is going on until they are told without any prior consultation. The group tends to stick together, it does not readily allow anyone else to belong to it, and its members back each other up. This is the way in which political infiltration has often worked. Once a small committed group gets power on a number of key committees they can exert an influence out of all proportion to their numbers. Such an abuse of openness and the inter-relations of the members of the body of Christ has often taken place within churches and in other Christian organisations. Sometimes this begins with the best of intentions. There are those who want to get things done, and they may achieve things that are very laudable and worthwhile. If this is the way it is done, however, there will be a price to pay in the end.

A problem which we have touched on arises where leaders appear to get almost detached from those who they are supposed to be leading. Some leaders seem to think that it is a necessary part of leadership to be remote and aloof. There may be various reasons for this; sometimes it is the protection of their position, at others it may be because they fear they will not be able to lead unless it is clearly seen that they are leaders. This has to be wrong because it is so unlike the pattern seen in the life of Jesus Christ.

He went out of his way to be approachable, 'Come to me, all you who are weary and burdened, and I will give you rest. Take my yoke upon you and learn from me, for I am gentle and humble in heart, and you will find rest for your souls. For my yoke is easy and my burden is light' (Matthew 11:28-30). The evidence of the Gospels is that a great variety of people came to Jesus, from many different walks of life. He did not turn them away. He was not brusque or impatient with them. He rebuked the disciples when they thought he would not want to be pestered by the mothers bringing their children to him. Christian leaders must be approachable by those in their care, and must talk freely and in a friendly fashion with them. Respect is not earned by adopting a stiff and starchy manner which scarcely deigns to notice others, but by obvious love, care and high qualities of life.

PASTOR, ELDERS AND DEACONS

It has to be admitted with sadness that one of the problem areas concerns the relationship between pastor and elders, or pastor and deacons where there are no elders. Aspects of this have been covered already. Sometimes the real problem has been the attitude of the pastor; the desire for position rather than service, or a steam-roller approach which does not consult or take account of the opinions of other leaders. Equally the fault is sometimes that of the elders (or deacons; circumstances differ in various churches, but from now on reference will only be made to other elders. What is said here can be applied to the various ways in which church leadership is arranged). Other elders sometimes seem to think they have been appointed to tell the pastor what he ought to do, or to act as a perpetual restraint because he cannot be trusted to take any wise decisions. Sometimes there appears to be sheer childishness in relationships between the two. Pastor and elders are supposed to work together in the gospel, they are to support each other and give themselves to the welfare of the whole body. If elders want a *pastor*, there is no point in appointing one and then trying to make him into a puppet. If a pastor knows there are other elders, or has others appointed while he is in office, then it is clear that he must work with them and not simply act as if they did not exist.

The office of pastor

This assumes that there is a distinct office of pastor; something which is not admitted by everyone. However, most churches which are large enough, do in fact have a pastor. Larger churches may have more than one. Generally speaking pastors are in the full employ of the church and especially have responsibility for preaching and teaching the Word of God. Without trying to establish the exact boundaries of responsibilities between pastors and other elders from the Bible, something which is difficult to do and possibly not even necessary, certain factors can be considered which show where the sources of tension lie. Understanding these may help to relieve that tension between leaders.

It is surely a fact of life that it is not possible for any group to function without having its own leader. This is a biblical principle which applies in all areas of life. In marriage and the family the husband is the head. The state has its authorities to whom we must submit. The church has its leaders. But amongst a group of leaders someone has to take the lead, at least when they meet together. Chairmanship has already been considered. Generally speaking even if the pastor does not chair meetings he should be seen to give spiritual direction and a spiritual lead, especially in directing the meeting to the Word of God. He is the one who teaches the church and the leadership and the members need to follow the teaching that is publicly given. It is an impossible situation if the pastor teaches one thing and there is resistance to it on the part of any the other leaders. While absolute unanimity on every point cannot be expected a pastor must be able to expound the Word according to the light he has and receive support from his fellow leaders. Known areas of disagreement on minor issues should be avoided in public ministry.

Parity of elders

Some difficulties arise because of the teaching that all elders are equal, or should be equal. Quite apart from the fact that this is not really possible in any case, it is certainly true that it simply creates trouble if the parity of elders is attempted in a situation where there is a pastor and elders. In nearly all cases like this there is no real parity and an attempt to act as if there was is a great mistake. There is often a completely different procedure used to appoint a pastor from that used to appoint the elders. There is much greater care taken over the choice of a pastor; it is a longer process and much more is expected in terms of training and preparation. Then it is frequently the case that church members think of a pastor in a different way to the other elders. Whatever they may be taught to think, if they have been used to the usual idea of a pastor they will not readily accept the idea of a body of elders as all equal. It may also be very difficult for a pastor to change his mind on this matter. Most pastors felt a call originally to a distinct pastoral office, to preaching and leading a church. In the majority of cases a pastor will have gone through some form of training, often college training, usually over several years. This may well have involved him in some sacrifice, perhaps considerable sacrifice. He may well feel that his sacrifice and training is being undervalued if he is simply looked upon as just another elder. A pastor is usually supported financially by the church. In this respect he is in a very different position to other elders, a position in which he may well feel rather vulnerable.

In drawing attention to these factors the point is not to say that there should be an absolute distinction between a pastor and other elders; it is to say that these constitute very considerable differences which need to be reckoned with. It is of course possible to envisage a leadership in which there is a much closer parity. There are some churches where this is so. In these cases the elders are quite often actually called pastors; perhaps a pastor with one or two assistant pastors, or a youth pastor. They are all chosen in the same way, and while they may not all have been to college they have either had some training or they undergo some while they are in office. They are also supported by the church. It looks rather as if the New Testament expected all elders to be supported in this way (see Acts 6:2; presumably the apostles formed the oversight of the Jerusalem church at that time). It is not difficult to imagine how a pastor might feel when he has to bear the brunt of the ministry on perhaps a fairly small stipend, and finds himself criticised or overridden by other elders who do very little practical ministry and may be earning two or three times what he does. Such a feeling is wrong, but we are exploring tensions, and we cannot overlook something like this.

Perhaps the matter of training and dedication is the most important. There is no parity at all between a man who has devoted himself for twenty years or so to the study of God's Word, who has long experience of pastoral ministry, and who has given up the prospect of a secular career at the call of Christ, and an elder who follows a secular calling and does his best for the church in his spare time. This is not in any way to disparage such an elder, he may be a man of true spirituality and godliness, of great value in the church. It is simply that there is qualitative difference between a pastor and an elder in these circumstances. Unless this is recognised there is likely to be trouble.

CALLING AND APPOINTMENT

Many problems arise because leaders are chosen for the wrong reasons. Some of these may be very understandable in the circumstances, but wrong reasons must be resisted. For example, there are some leaders who get appointed ultimately as a reward for long membership or long service in the church. They have been in a church for a long time and it seems almost wrong to overlook them for leadership and appoint those who have been in the church for a much shorter time, or who are much younger men. Yet this outlook cannot be right, because it means that virtually every man who stays in the church long enough will eventually get to the leadership. In fact leadership may come to be thought of some higher status that is the right of all older men in the church. Such an attitude overlooks the fact that the Lord gives gifts to people for different forms of service. It means that younger men will virtually never be appointed to leadership, and that those without suitable gifts will eventually be put in a position for which they are not equipped. Moreover, having waited long until they were elevated to the leadership they are not likely to want to retire from it, and will take it as a personal insult if there is any suggestion they should step down.

It has sometimes been suggested that a person should be made a leader in order to get him active in the church, or perhaps to try and restrain him from criticising the leadership, or to curtail the awkward questions he asks in the church meeting. These are clearly totally inadequate reasons for such appointment. A person who is not doing very much in the church may well need to be stirred up and perhaps given some responsibility, but it is those who are already showing their gifts and who are actively showing initiative in service who should be considered for leadership. Those with a critical spirit should not be considered for leadership, but those who show independence of thought, and who recall the church to the Scriptures and whose questions are spiritual and searching, should certainly not be written off as potential leaders because of these things. Such people may well be very valuable in a leadership, provided they have other suitable gifts.

Men may be appointed to leadership because they are very successful in their secular business. They are men of influence and it is thought that the church will gain credibility in the eyes of people around if it is known that they are leaders in it. They may be highly thought of in the local community and already serve on various committees. However these considerations are not relevant; if a man has spirituality and gifts then he should be appointed and his standing locally may be an asset. If he does not have the necessary spiritual qualifications then he must not be appointed. A man may be quite wealthy and people may feel that if he is appointed he will be more disposed to help the church financially. This is a dreadful reason for appointing someone to leadership among God's people.

People have been appointed because they have plenty of spare time, or because they get things done, or because they are yes men and will not oppose what others want to do, or because they are weak and are never going to challenge anyone or stir the church up if this is what it really needs. It is easy enough in theory to reject all such unworthy and worldly reasoning; church members need to examine their hearts and motives closely when it comes to the appointment of leaders to make sure that such considerations do not underlie the choices they make.

Manner of appointment

The way in which leaders are appointed is important too. Churches vary about how they do this. It is not necessary here to try and prescribe an exact way of doing things, but it is surely evident that the existing leaders ought to have a major part in the process, though the final appointing must involve the approval of the church. It is doubtful whether it is a good thing simply to have a nomination process which is open to any member. There have been churches in which unsuitable men have been nominated year after year by their friends—presumably!—only to suffer the humiliation of consistently failing to be voted into office. There is a better way of doing things than that. It is surely evident that only those who have the necessary qualities and gifts should ever be put forward for leadership. Those who are already leaders have to be very careful of bias, or of not wanting the status quo to be disturbed, but they should surely only allow suitable names to be brought before the church. However names need to be brought before the church, at least for ratification. It is pointless to appoint a leader who does not have the confidence of the main body of the membership. The important thing is to have a procedure which is sensitive to these considerations and to ensure that everything is done in a prayerful and spiritual manner.

Another thorny issue is the length of service to which leaders are appointed. In some churches leaders stand for election or re-election every year, in other churches they are not appointed for any fixed term at all. There are some benefits in having election for a fixed term: though one year does seem too short. For example, it means that if a man proves unsuitable, or finds he cannot cope with the demands of leadership, he simply does not stand for re-election. However this does seem to place the emphasis in the wrong place. If the Lord has given gifts of leadership to men, and the church recognises that this is so, why does this have to be re-affirmed every three years? Doesn't it give the impression that men can do their stint on the leadership for a term or two, and then give others a turn? Churches have to work this out for themselves, but they need to think things through carefully. There does need to be provision for the removal of unsatisfactory leaders, but leaders are a gift from Christ to be recognised and given authority to serve the Lord in the church.

Preparation for leadership

Another matter connected with appointment is preparation for leadership. May a man have gifts and potential and yet be unready for service? Does there need to be some preparation before a man is appointed to leadership? This has been covered in chapter 7. The point to be considered here is this. Isn't it true that some of the difficulties that arise both between leaders themselves and leaders and the church come from lack of forethought and a failure to understand how leaders are to function? People can be gifted, and yet not use their gifts correctly. They can have knowledge yet not understand how to apply their knowledge to actual situations. Their principles may be biblical and right, yet they may not easily relate to other people, and in leadership this is very important.

Two solutions can be offered here. First of all, Christians who are concerned to serve the Lord should try to develop their gifts as much as they can, and they should also try to develop their ability to converse with and be a spiritual help to other members of the church. Potential leaders often look for opportunities to preach or to lead Bible studies, but they do not always seem to realise the opportunities that are all around them with regard to personal relations and spiritual conversation. Talking and visiting can be done by any believer, and as this is done leadership gifts reveal themselves. Those who are the right material for leadership will already be taking some steps to prepare themselves. Secondly, the existing leadership should help potential leaders to develop. This may not be with a direct intention that a particular person should become a leader, but if general preparation is given this is a help to start with. Those who are appointed to leadership could be encouraged, perhaps required, to take a correspondence course, or go on a training course in the principles of leadership.

STATUS WITHOUT MINISTRY

Whether we like it or not leadership brings a certain status to those who exercise it. In many cases respect is earned, and those who are leaders are to be highly respected for the work's sake. Yet because we are still in an imperfect condition, status can go to our heads; this can happen to any one of us. Status can be secretly desired for its own sake—and not just by the person concerned, but by wives, children and other family members and friends. It can be frankly enjoyed, any position which gives us some prominence and elevates us above our peers can give a certain inner satis-faction and smugness. It can be something which we do not want to give up, and which we will cling on to if at all possible. This is a spiritual disease which has to be remedied by those biblical considerations, and sometimes providential circumstances, which keep us humble and remind us we are called to serve, not to preen ourselves before others.

However it appears that in not a few churches leaders do not appear actually to have any specific ministries, and this can be a problem. Within most churches there are those with specific responsibilities; treasurer and secretary are obvious ones. But there are other leaders, they may be deacons or elders, or both, who do not have any particular function to perform. They attend leaders' meetings, but it does not appear that they have any other function, nor in some cases does it appear that they think they have any.

This may make it appear as if a place on the leadership is something which is likely to be given to every man in the church in due time, there is nothing you actually do except out of your experience contribute to the leaders' meetings. In some cases men do not even make any great contribution to the discussion in their meetings. Most meetings tend to be dominated by a few who are articulate and who have thought out their position on most issues which arise, while others are for the most part content to listen and generally to agree.

This leads to a rather delicate point. When should leaders retire, or be retired, or, if that is the system, no longer stand for re-election? The difficulty is that if leaders think more in terms of status than anything else, they will be reluctant to retire, nor will they see any reason to do so. Moreover people in the church will say things like, "Fancy asking Mr X to retire from the leadership after all the service he has given to the church over the years!" This simply indicates that leadership is not thought of in terms of service, but rather of status and reward. The point is not that those who have served well should not have recognition for that, clearly they should, but that the point of leadership is to lead and to serve, and if a person is no longer able to do that, then it is difficult to see why he should continue on the leadership. The same applies if a person's health becomes bad, or his circumstances change and he can no longer give adequate time. It is not a matter of wanting to demote anyone, or of not being kind. Leadership is a high and demanding calling, and this must be recognised and followed through in the church.

Does this mean that every leader should have a specific responsibility? Not necessarily; though it may be a good thing to give leaders areas of responsibility in the work of the church according to their gifts. It does mean, however, that leaders should see themselves as workers, and example-setters. They need to take meetings seriously, and realise they have a responsibility to contribute where they can. Experience tends to show that often when a rather quieter or more reticent leader is asked his opinion he has a very useful contribution to make, which modesty, or perhaps the fact that others are always having their say, keeps him from saying without being prompted. They should also take the lead in speaking with people in the church, in welcoming visitors, in being available to church members who want to say something to the leadership. There are many informal ways in which leaders can fulfil their functions without being given specific responsibilities. However they must ensure they do these things. Many who are appointed to leadership will already have various responsibilities in the church.

Probably more could be made of giving responsibility to leaders. In many churches where there is a pastor too much is usually left to him. To give some specific suggestions. One leader could have general oversight of the young peoples' work. It would probably help if he was involved in that anyway, but it is not essential. Those involved in this work would then know they could always speak to him; he would be their liaison with the leaders. Moreover, he could look in from time to time, not to spy, or make the leaders feel uncomfortable, but to encourage them, give them support, take some part in the programme, make them feel the leadership is behind them and wants to give them every encouragement and help. He could also attend some of the meetings of the leaders of that work. Another leader could be given the responsibility of noticing people who are absent from services, of finding out those who are unwell and passing on the names of those who need visiting. All this will prevent the feeling that leadership is a matter of position; everyone will see that it is a matter of ministry.

DEMARCATION OF MINISTRIES

This raises another area where difficulties can arise. Leaders can become somewhat sensitive about their own tasks and resent others who appear to interfere. If a man has been given a task he may feel he should be left to get on with it; he may even become rather reluctant to say much about it at leaders' meetings. This means that the leaders should have some guidelines which are understood by all. If responsibilities are shared out then they should be reasonably clearly defined. While there is often a certain overlap, it is frustrating if two men are trying to do much the same sort of thing independently. It is certainly likely to lead to unnecessary friction.

Similarly there should be some understanding about what is left to the leader to get on with and what should be brought to the leaders' meeting for discussion. Some leaders' meetings get bogged down with unnecessary details. On the other hand the overall responsibility for the whole church belongs to the whole leadership and they need to be informed about all the main matters. Leaders need to be given a certain independence to get on with their own responsibility, yet when necessary the whole leadership may discuss a particular problem or need. The leader concerned should not feel threatened by this; he acts in his responsibility on behalf of all the leaders so when necessary they will discuss matters with him.

AGE OF LEADERS

Many leaderships will be made up of men with an age range of thirty years or so. It is certainly best if there is a good span of years as this means there are men with experience and also those who are in touch with the way younger people think and who are being prepared for service in years to come. The very word 'elder' suggests a certain maturity and experience, without putting a definite age on it. However, it is possible for men in their twenties to have these qualities, so, though this may be unusual, churches should not automatically exclude younger men from their thinking. However, there are problems associated both with youth and age. This was considered earlier in a more general way, but it is important to look at it from the point of view of leadership.

Youth

The first and most obvious temptation of younger men is pride. Paul warns Timothy that those recently converted should not be made elders for this reason, 'he must not be a recent convert, or he may become conceited and fall under the same judgment as the devil' (1 Timothy 3:6). This can easily be the case with a younger man, too, even though he may have been converted several years earlier. However in that case his conversion will have taken place while he was still a teenager if not earlier, and most people mature later than that. Young men with real gifts who could have made a valuable contribution to the life of the church have allowed the fact that they have been brought into leadership positions or given opportunities to preach to go to their heads and thus deprived the church, if not positively harmed it, and have also spoilt their own Christian life, at least for a while. The expression, 'It takes a steady hand to hold a full cup' is very true. George Whitefield's remarkable ministry began when he was very young, and we find him writing like this when he was twenty-two; 'The tide of popularity now began to run very high. In a short time, I could no longer walk on foot as usual, but was constrained to go in a coach, from place to place, to avoid the hosannas of the multitude. They grew quite extravagant in their applauses; and, had it not been for my compassionate High Priest, popularity would have destroyed me. I used to plead with him, to take me by the hand and lead me through this fiery furnace. He heard my request, and gave me to see the vanity of all commendations but his own.' (*George Whitefield's Journals*, Banner of Truth Trust, p.89). God may take and use men while they are very young; but they must always watch out for pride. Those who had far less reason than Whitefield have grievously fallen in this respect.

Younger men will almost inevitably lack experience. They may know more of Scripture than older men, but they will not have experience of how Scripture is to be applied and worked out in the church. Their knowledge, therefore, will be more theoretical. They will have less understanding of the human heart; both their own and those of others. They do not realise the subtlety of the devil in attacking leaders, and leaderships, nor are they always aware of how devious and sometimes downright deceitful people in churches can be. The depravity of the heart is not just a doctrinal belief, it is painfully discovered to be a reality by those who are called to leadership.

Younger men tend to be prone to impatience also. This is a difficult matter. Some leaderships drag their heels terribly. Drive and enthusiasm are clearly good qualities to have. Yet it is also true that a great deal of harm has been done by energetic Christians who have rushed into doing things without counting the cost, or considering whether it is possible to finish what has been started. In any case it is no good if leaders rush on far in front of those they are supposed to be leading. The whole essence of leadership is to be able to carry other people with you. Prayerful patience is always a needed quality amongst Christian leaders.

Younger men can also sometimes be disparaging about their elders, and sometimes disrespectful and rude. This is often when their patience has run out; when they feel that older men are simply blocking the way to progress. This fault is serious on several counts. It is a biblical principle that older people are to be respected, and in days when those who are older are easily written off as 'wrinklies' it is important for Christians to resist the spirit of the age. This also sets a very bad example to other younger people in the church. As we have seen, example is particularly important for leaders. It is bad for any Christian to behave like this, but on a leadership it is likely to sour relationships and prevent the leaders from working together as a team.

Age

There are temptations that face older leaders as well. Unfortunately pride can afflict them almost as easily. It is sometimes pride which makes them reluctant to admit younger men on to the leadership. It is pride that makes them feel they have always got to assert their opinions. It is pride that makes them feel they are almost indispensable to the working of the church.

Older men can get blinkered in their views; they can find it hard to understand new times and new ways of doing things. Living as we do in a time when change happens more quickly than it has ever done before means it is very difficult for any of us to keep pace with what is happening. It is not so easy to be flexible or adaptable when one is older, and yet these are vital qualities, though they must be exercised within biblical parameters.

MALE AND FEMALE IN THE CHURCH

This is not a section about the issues raised by feminism; it was a problem area long before modern questions were being raised. Neither am I thinking at this point of the problems raised by relationships between the sexes in the fellowship of the church. It is true that many churches have experienced problems at this point. Sometimes this is because of a naivety which assumes that Christians are not tempted as other people are. It is surprising how those who profess belief in total depravity can falsify their creed by their foolish behaviour which exposes to temptation.

Leaders and their wives

It has been obvious, but unstated, that this book assumes that leadership in the church is male. Certainly it is clear from the New Testament that elders and preachers are to be men; the evidence regarding deacons is more uncertain. However, this does not mean that women have no influence over what leaders decide. It is not unusual for a leader to express the feeling that a decision ought not to be made at a particular meeting because, in reality, he wants to consult his wife before he makes up his mind. In some cases men dare not make up their minds until they have made sure that their wives will approve of the decision. It is one thing for a married man—and not all leaders are married, nor do they have to be—to discuss church matters with his wife in a spiritual and prayerful manner; this is part of what it means to be united in marriage. It is quite another if such discussion is motivated by personal weakness, or fear of what his wife might think and say. The wives of leaders must be absolutely trustworthy and able to keep any confidence which husbands place in them. This is not always the case, and unfortunately some churches have suffered because of a leakage of leadership matters via the wives of leaders. There may even be some matters that leaders should not share with their wives. Although the words of 1 Timothy 3:4,5, 'He must manage his own family well and see that his children obey him with proper respect. (If anyone does not know how to manage his own family, how can he take care of God's church?)' do not primarily have the husband/wife relationship in view, it is clear that they include it. The position of a man in his own family must be taken into account before he is appointed to leadership, and this must include his relationship with his wife. In some cases a wife may not be a believer at all, or not established as a believer or very spiritually-minded. This does not absolutely prevent a man from becoming a leader, but it does mean that he cannot talk with his wife about church matters in the way that another leader might.

Women's ministries

The main problem here arises because churches do not always have the biblical provision for teaching and guiding women members within the church. There are several passages in Scripture which are important here. In Titus 2:3-5 Paul speaks about the example and role of older women in the church. They have an important ministry towards the younger women, particularly in teaching them to live as Christians within the home. In 1 Timothy 5:9,10 there is a reference to a list of widows who appear to exercise some form of ministry within the church, while at the same time being provided for by the church. There is also the enigmatic reference to 'women' in the description of the qualities which are appropriate for deacons (1 Timothy 3:11; NIV has 'wives' in the text and 'deaconesses' in the margin). A good case can be made for understanding the word to refer to female deacons (see Sharon James, 'Roles without Relegation' in *Men, Women and Authority*, Day One, pp.241-243). It is likely that it is because deacons have taken on some of the responsibilities of elders that deaconesses have fallen out of favour in most churches. Another possible reason is that originally deacons, male and female, may have been simply servants of the church with a variety of responsibilities, while more recently the diaconate has been formalised as an office with regular meetings, and annual or triennial voting for its membership.

The result is that in most churches aspects of the care the church should have towards its women are very much of an *ad hoc* nature. It is often assumed that the pastor's wife will have a leading role among the women, though there is no more reason why this should be so than there is for an accountant's wife to be able to deal with the financial affairs of his female clients. That the wives of many pastors do, in fact, fulfil a very valuable role in the church only makes it more difficult for those who feel their only calling is to be a wife and mother. Moreover where does a pastor's wife turn if she wants to discuss a matter which would be most appropriately discussed with another woman? What is important is that the many areas in which women can serve, and in some cases in which only they can serve, should be adequately covered.

Pastoral counselling

One aspect which needs to be looked at in more detail is the pastoral counselling of women within the church. There is no reason to suppose that there is a greater need for this than there is for the counselling of men, in fact if we take seriously the headship of the husband in the family then it is the men who primarily need biblical guidance in the fulfilling of their responsibilities in the home. However, many churches have more women in them than men, and sadly marriages do come under strain so that both husbands and wives need help and counsel. This raises a number of difficulties. For example, some pastors either fall into adultery or leave their wives because they have become involved with women they started off trying to help, usually women whose own marriages were under strain. Also some wives, whose marriages are in difficulty, feel that they have not been understood, or their side of the story not appreciated, because it has always been a couple of male elders from the church who have visited, listened and given counsel.

I do not intend to try to give any direct instructions to solve these problems. Each leadership, each church, needs to consider these matters themselves. The last thing I want to do is to set off a debate about the exact interpretation of 1 Timothy 3:11, for example. However, it can be said that as a general rule male leaders should not visit women alone, or see them on their own, with the exception of those of an advanced age. In dealing with marriage problems, or matters of alleged immorality, the sensitivities of women must be recognised and it is almost essential that a suitable woman (or women) is involved in the process of pastoral help and discipline. In addition the church needs to use women with suitable gifts in a wide range of care, from teenagers anxious about sexual matters, to young wives, singles, marriage help, and more practical help especially with the elderly and handicapped. This cannot be an entirely separate area of church life, cut off from the overall pastoral care exercised by the leadership—as quite often happens—so links must be made and fostered which enable the church to minister to all its members and to be prepared for all the difficulties which might arise.

While pastors' wives, and the wives of other leaders may often be able to meet the needs mentioned above, this should not just be assumed. In some cases they may not be suitable, or they may not wish to be involved; and there may be other women in the church who are suitable, the modern-day equivalents of the 'elder women' and 'widows' mentioned in the letters to Titus and Timothy. With the increase of marriage problems and divorce today it is more necessary to give attention to this problem area than was the case in the past.

QUESTIONS FOR STUDY AND DISCUSSION

1. How would your church go about calling: a) a pastor b) an elder?

2. Being realistic, what qualities would you look for in a pastor?

3. What do you understand is involved in spiritual oversight?

4. What ministries need to be performed by women in your church?

5. Case study: What principles can you find in 1 Corinthians 6:1-6 for dealing with problems in a church?

Restoring harmony

Paul begins the last chapter of Galatians like this, "Brothers, if someone is caught in a sin, you who are spiritual should restore him gently. But watch yourself, or you also may be tempted. Carry each other's burdens and in this way fulfil the law of Christ." It is not easy to restore Christians who have fallen into sin, nor to reconcile those who have fallen out with each other. Paul calls upon those who are spiritual to do this work. Certainly it needs spirituality to be able to do it; an attitude which comes from the Spirit of Christ living in the heart. Those who engage in it have to be gentle. It may not be easy to be gentle with brothers or sisters whose own attitudes may be very wrong or stubborn. Yet it is the soft answer which turns away anger and enables you to get alongside those who need restoring. Those who do this must also watch out for themselves. It is so easy to take sides, to lose one's objectivity and one's cool! Many temptations lie in wait for those who think they can restore their fellow believers. They must carry other people's burdens, get involved in their troubles and hurts, sometimes giving practical help. In this way they fulfil the law of Christ. All this must be borne in mind as this chapter proceeds.

HEALING BROKEN RELATIONSHIPS

How many difficulties can arise when trying to heal broken relationships! Often people express a willingness to be reconciled—the problem, they say, is always with the other party. It takes wisdom and grace to work through the problems.

Misunderstandings

Many relationships break down as a result of misunderstandings, and many are difficult to restore simply because all sorts of misunderstandings have arisen after the original problem. People can also be very sensitive on this point. They often feel their judgment is being questioned if it is suggested they have failed to understand what another said, or meant. Neither do they always like it if it is pointed out to them that something they said or did could easily have been misunderstood. There is no easy way to help iron out misunderstandings.

Perhaps of prime importance is a teaching ministry which reminds everyone of the way in which we can all misunderstand others. We are all sinful people, and we have our own prejudices. We need to realise it is very easy for us to get things wrong. This does not mean we are to become unsure of everything we think and have no firm opinions at all, nor that we are always trying to fit in with what other people say they meant or did. It does mean we must think carefully, that we must try to evaluate what we hear, that we must be ready to listen to what other people say, though we reserve the right to come to our own conclusions. All this is a part of wisdom, and it grows by experience.

What we must avoid are hasty judgments. It is true that some Christian leaders develop the gift of quickly seeing the heart of a matter. God gives them a gift of discernment which is of great value. Yet usually this is developed as a result of careful observation, the asking of probing questions, and a knowledge of the ways the human heart works. Many others rush to judgment, and having once committed themselves to a point of view are very reluctant to change their minds. It is not surprising that Cromwell once said, "I beseech you in the bowels of Christ to consider yourselves mistaken."

One reason for misunderstanding is that people's perceptions of the same event can differ greatly. This can be so with the most ordinary of happenings. We all look at things from our own particular perspective, and this can lead to apparent discrepancies of fact. Added to this it is so difficult to know how other people feel. If only we could get inside the skin of the other person we would know why he spoke as he did! Of course; and here is another problem, some people try to hide behind misunderstanding. They never lie, they never distort the truth, it's just that they are misunderstood!

Suspicion and lack of trust

One of the reasons for misunderstanding, and one of the difficulties in disposing of it when it occurs, is that once people have fallen out with one other, they often become very suspicious of each other. It has to be acknowledged with sadness that far too many Christians are suspicious of their brothers and sisters in Christ. There is an attitude of mistrust in too many churches, and people seem to be on the look out for heresy or points for which they can criticise. Part of the reason for this is the great changes which have come into some churches; ministers and others changing their opinions and practice and trying to compel everyone to follow their lead. There have also been all sorts of novel ideas, unscriptural practices, dubious teachings which have made Christians hyper-sensitive, and unsure even of people they once respected and trusted.

Christian people are not to be naïve, the Bible teaching on the depravity of the human heart ought to rule that out, yet it is better to be naïve and trusting than eaten up with suspicion. If there cannot be trust within the fellowship of Christian people, where can it exist? The fact is that we can generally trust our brothers and sisters, and we ought to believe what they say unless we have definite grounds for doubting it. When quarrels arise people begin to doubt the good will of others. Instead of thinking of their brothers as fallible Christians who need help and constructive criticism (just as we all do), they feel they are awkward, wilfully difficult and never likely to change. Sometimes, of course, this proves to be true; sometimes it becomes pretty clear that a person is not a Christian at all. However, it is quite wrong to be suspecting that nearly everyone you fall out with is really an unbeliever. Within the church we must help each other to sort out problems and relationship difficulties, to learn to apologise and to forgive. Leaders are to set a clear example in these things.

Entrenched positions

It is particularly difficult when a problem has gone on for a long time and people have taken up entrenched positions. In such cases there may not seem to be a problem at all, for it is well hidden. Gradually, however, it becomes apparent that a breakdown in relationships in the past was never dealt with and healed. A *modus vivendi* was arrived at. The persons concerned learnt how to get on with each other in a polite way, avoiding any close contact, and never working together. Other people, whether they really knew about the problem or not, adjusted to the situation. Many a new pastor has come to discover such situations as he has got to know the members of his church. If he then tries to do something about the situation he is looked upon as someone who is disturbing the peace, stirring up the past, raking up old problems. However, if they affect relationships in the present then they are not simply old problems which can lie forgotten.

Where this happens, those who have refused to put things right have almost invariably stopped growing as Christians in the particular area of the problem. If one of them has a character trait which causes problems to fellow believers, instead of it being challenged, brought out into the open so that it can be mortified, it will rather be reinforced. This is probably true of large numbers of Christians. They justify their character or temperamental weaknesses, never allowing these to be challenged or brought to the Lord for change, and as a result there is no alteration or progress in that area of their life at all. This can be just as true of leaders as of the rest of the membership.

Some 'entrenched positions' are absolutely right. It was correct for Athanasius to stand against the world, when it was becoming Arian. In many churches it is a good thing when believers stand for fundamental truths and for godly principles. Yet even here attitudes are important. It is possible to make a stand for undoubted truth in a way which neither honours God nor commends the truth to others. It requires love and tact to approach and help Christians to see that the positions they have adopted are wrong, at least in attitude. To winkle some out of their dugouts and into a godly love and fellowship within the church can be a very taxing exercise, yet it must be attempted.

Facing the facts

It is easy enough to acknowledge that the 'heart is deceitful above all things and beyond cure. Who can understand it?' It is another thing to recognise that this is also true of my heart. It is very unpleasant to have pointed out to me ways in which I have deceived myself, or facts about myself which I would rather not believe are true, or facts about a situation or person which I have judged quite differently. It is extraordinary how reluctant some people are to face what are obvious facts if looked at honestly.

It is not uncommon where there has been a breakdown of relationships to find that there is actual conflict over matters of fact. A leader will talk to one person for his story, and then to the other and find there is real disagreement over what happened or what was said. Sometimes this is a matter of things being seen from one point of view, sometimes it is exaggeration, the result of dwelling on one aspect so much that it has grown in the mind. It can be a matter of having forgotten what actually did happen; at times there may be deliberate lying. Those who have tried to help partners where a marriage has broken down will know how difficult it can be to get to the truth.

Within churches it must be emphasised that believers must speak the truth. God is a God who cannot lie, and those who belong to him are committed to truthfulness. What happens is that people are very sensitive about any suggestion that what they are saying may not be actually what happened, but they are not nearly as sensitive about being absolutely sure that they remember the facts and tell them without elaboration. We are not to expect people to be pedantically accurate in all they say, but some people are very careless about they way in which they speak and some constantly exaggerate. Some also say much too much, especially about other people. All this makes for problems, and is likely to contribute to relationship difficulties.

Losing face

We live in a world in which people desire to keep their pride, and as a result, look upon losing face as a great evil to be avoided at all costs. It is for this reason that many people will not admit to things they have said or done, or will not repent, or only make apologies which are not far from being self-justifications for their actions. Yet a great deal of this is simply wrong-headed from a Christian point of view. For Christians, acknowledging sins and making apology are not matters of losing face at all. We all know this. We respect the person who is prepared to come clean and who is prepared to make a proper apology when this is necessary. Such a person goes up in our estimation, not down.

Many Christians need to be helped to see the importance of honest confession. Even in confessing our sins to the Lord it is very easy to frame our prayer so as to excuse what we have done, or add explanations. In confessing and apologising to brothers and sisters in the Lord it is even easier to do the same. Ken Sande's book referred to earlier has an excellent chapter on this. One section is entitled, 'Avoid If, But, and Maybe'. His examples are very telling: 'I'm sorry *if* I've done something to upset you.' 'I shouldn't have lost my temper, *but* I was tired.' '*Maybe* I could have tried harder' (*The Peacemaker,* p.96,97). It is this sort of blurring of the issues and refusal to face what we've said or done which actually causes us to lose face before others. Fellow Christians are not taken in by this half-hearted type of apology.

It is possible for those who are receiving an apology to help those making it. On one occasion I was trying to apologise to a much older Christian. I was rather frightened at the ordeal and stumbling over my words, when he said, kindly but firmly, 'What is it you're really trying to say?' That enabled me simply to say what was necessary without any further fuss.

When leaders in the church are trying to bring about reconciliation, or dealing with someone who has fallen into sin, it is important for them to remember that they are not out to humiliate anyone, nor unnecessarily to expose them in public. Not all believers seem to understand this. Peter reminds us that 'love covers over a multitude of sins' (1 Peter 4:8), and this is an important principle. In this sense we should be concerned not to make people lose face before their fellow believers. It is true that Paul says of elders, 'Those who sin are to be warned publicly, so that the others may take warning', but this is a special case. Clearly if leaders sin, it is necessary to take measures to counteract the extremely damaging example that has been set. Both the world and the church need to know that sin in a leader is taken very seriously. Even here, however, there is no intent to humiliate, and there should be no exaggeration of what has happened, nor using it for a personal attack on the individual concerned. The only concern is for people to learn to avoid the sin themselves.

Refusing to apologise

Regrettably this is not all that uncommon. Of course there are a number of reasons why people are not prepared to confess their fault, apologise for it and ask for forgiveness. Often it is because they do not believe they have done, or said, anything wrong. In some cases this may be true. However, if another person has been hurt then, even if it was done unintentionally and perhaps without any real sin being involved, they should certainly be anxious to do all they can to restore right relationships. Sometimes people will not apologise because they think the other person is simply making a fuss about nothing. Often this itself is a symptom of a broken relationship. On the one hand one person has become over-sensitive, on the other there is a hardness and dismissiveness of the first. People refuse to apologise because they think the other person was in the wrong, or was to blame first, or is the more blameworthy. In these circumstances they will only apologise if the other does so first.

There is a childishness about all this, and yet these attitudes are very common. They raise a question about the relationship to God of the person who refuses to apologise. Every day believers have to express their sorrow to God for some sin or other. It is of the very essence of walking humbly with God to confess our sins to him and sorrow over the way we fall into temptation and over the many unworthy attitudes we display. How can Christians keep short accounts with God and yet refuse to express a proper sorrow and regret to their fellow believers when they have hurt and grieved them? The short answer is that this is not possible; the refusal to deal openly with a brother is an index to a heart that is wrong with the Lord himself. Leaders need to be firm in pointing this out when trying to bring Christians together.

When there is a clear refusal to apologise and put right a wrong then the situation is the one envisaged in Matthew 18:15,16. In these circumstances it may be necessary to follow the steps on to v.18, and for the person who will not face their sin to be put out of the fellowship of the church. It must be clearly understood that the reason for this is not the original fault, which may not in itself be particularly serious. However, refusing to respond to the loving appeals of fellow believers and finally of the church itself is serious. This sort of stubbornness contradicts the whole basis of Christian fellowship and the discipline of the church, and can only be met by exclusion, though even this hopes for, and intends, the restoration of the person concerned.

Spiritual blackmail

Perhaps this would be better described as 'unspiritual blackmail'. It does not simply occur when there are relational problems within a church, it is all too often a feature of church life. By spiritual blackmail I mean those occasions when people try to get their own way by threatening either to give up their particular responsibility or to leave the church altogether.

Some people seem to develop a 'threatening to resign' syndrome. As a result the rest of the church, and the leadership, are constantly on tenterhooks. Everyone knows that it is important not to upset Mr X or Mrs Y. As a result they are allowed much too much influence in the church and the opinions and convictions of other, quieter—more gracious?—members are not taken into account as they ought to be. This is not true fellowship. This is not how the church should act as a body, caring for all the members and taking into account the views of all.

It is not easy to deal with such a state of affairs. Leaders have occasionally called the bluff of such people and if they have decided to leave, the rest of the church has heaved a sigh of relief. This may be understandable, but it is not the best way. It is neither in the interests of the church nor those who have left. Not infrequently people have left churches in this way to their own great loss. In the end they tend to wander from church to church, never finding a spiritual home they feel they can settle in. We can only hope that in God's mercy they reach a heavenly home in the end.

Part of the problem is the fragmented state of church life in these days, and the mindset that we have allowed ourselves to fall into which says that faithfulness to the Lord means ensuring that our own convictions are insisted upon whatever other brothers in the Lord think. This has been covered in the earlier part of the book. On the one hand clear teaching needs to be given from the Word of God, and the unspiritual devices believers can fall into exposed for what they are. On the other hand there needs to be proper pastoral care of these people and fellowship with them. Often people tend to avoid them, and this makes the situation worse. At times they are concerned about real issues, issues which others may not have thought through, or on which others are not as firm as they ought to be. If that is so then they need to realise that the way to change the minds of their brothers and sisters is not by threatening to resign, but by prayer, by love, by explanation from the Scriptures, by their wholehearted involvement in the church as the body of believers to which the

Lord has joined them. In this the leaders are to assist by their understanding and care for the whole church.

QUALITIES FOR A PEACEMAKER

This section simply picks out some important features, emphasising some spiritual qualities which have already been mentioned, and touching on others which may be overlooked.

Dependence on God

Perhaps this is the most important of all. One of the dangers of leadership, or of trying to make peace, is that pride comes in and tells us that we are rather good at this sort of thing. If God seems to have given us a gift for getting alongside others and helping them in their problems, we start taking credit for ourselves. Conversely if we find we are unsuccessful in resolving a difficulty we say to ourselves, 'I ought to have been able to sort that out'! In this matter, as in many others, the words of Proverbs 3:5-7 are essential, 'Trust in the LORD with all your heart and lean not on your own understanding; in all your ways acknowledge him, and he will make your paths straight. Do not be wise in your own eyes; fear the LORD and shun evil.'

We need to remember that the church is Christ's, and so are all believers. As Shepherd and Head he has far greater insight and a far greater care for the churches than any of us do. He is building his church. It is he who will bring to completion the good work which he has started (Philippians 1:6). We can have too great a concern because we are leaving him out of our reckoning, or we can be too independent for the same reason. Who do we think *we* are anyway?

We know, too, that just as he walks among the churches (Revelation 2:1) so he also dwells in the hearts of those who are his. He is there to rule, to guide, to rebuke and to correct. God is the Father of his children and just as earthly fathers discipline their children and punish them when necessary, so our heavenly Father does the same, (Hebrews 12:5-11). We often lose sight of this. It may be due to our lack of spiritual understanding, but it is not easy to discern when troubles or difficulties are being used as chastisements. The fact is, though, that God does do this work when necessary. Leaders need to realise this too. In many cases it is not easy to be sure what discipline is necessary, or even whether action should be taken. We cannot read hearts or easily discern motives. But God can, and he takes the action he sees to be appropriate. It is not a light thing when he raises his hand against his disobedient children.

However while the Lord acts apart from leaders in the church—sometimes in spite of them!—he generally works through them, and through others whom he has equipped as peacemakers. We are instruments in the hand of Christ, and we can look to him for grace. We will not get very far unless we do depend on him. In sorting out problems and restoring relationships prayer is vital.

Knowledge of the Scriptures

It seems unnecessary to mention this, as it has been emphasised so often throughout this book. What needs to be stressed here though is the importance of a practical knowledge of Scripture. That is, being able to see how Scripture applies to different cases and being able effectively to do this. It is one thing to know doctrine, or to know the stories of Scripture. It is another to know how to take principles and apply them to all the problems that afflict churches and believers.

This starts with ourselves. When we know how to read the Scriptures in such a way that our own lives are corrected, reformed, redirected; when we know how to sort out our own problems, and to apply the Word to our own spiritual illnesses and weaknesses, then we are beginning to be in the position where we can help others. This, of course, is why the Lord so often brings potential leaders and those he is going to use through all sorts of troubles and difficulties. It is as they wrestle with these in the light of the Word of God that they are fashioned as shepherds and peacemakers. It is not enough just to read or study the Bible; rather we need to interact with it continually in our daily lives and so gain personal experience of the way it answers the problems and needs we encounter.

Along with this there has to be personal submission to Scripture as God's Word. That is implicit in what has been said, but it ought to be spelled out. I am more and more convinced that many problems are at root simple disobedience to the Word of God. All sorts of plausible reasons are given why a person thinks his case is special or why a biblical principle does not apply to his situation, but often the answer is just to obey. It is all too easy to try to elude the Word of God; to be less than honest in our dealings with the Lord as he speaks through his Word. The person who seeks to solve problems and reconcile believers who are alienated from each other must first be honest in submitting to the Word himself. In doing so he will begin to be made aware of the devices the human heart has for evading truth, and he will also approach a moral position in which he can honestly counsel others.

Desire for God's glory

This is of fundamental importance. Above and beyond the good of the church and its individual members is God's glory. So many things that happen in churches and between believers bring dishonour on the Lord. Yet, to be truthful, this is seldom the major consideration in many Christians' minds. If it was, half the problems wouldn't arise in the first place. It is very important for those who desire to help others to keep this in view. It is so easy to think of oneself; to want to prove oneself; or justify one's position as a leader; or maintain a reputation as a peacemaker. These very things actually detract from the glory of God. We do not serve Christ for our sakes, but for his glory.

The object is not to please people, even Christians. Many people can be hurt when relationships break down, or when there is strife in a church. But the object of the peacemaker is not just to restore relationships so that everyone feels happy again. Sometimes putting the glory of God first will mean that some people are not at all happy; they may be made very unhappy, at least for a while. It is not just a matter of bringing people together, nor of getting them to forget the past. Real sins have to be repented of. Apologies may have to be made. Full and frank forgiveness has to be extended. Some may have to face themselves and longstanding habits of disobedience. Some may find that the Word probes their lives, and demands discipline, correction, change. All this can be very painful. The glory of God demands nothing less. In the long run, of course, such pain is productive of great spiritual joy and peace.

Self-denying humility

Galatians 6:1 reminded us that restoration must be done gently. Proverbs

15:1 says, 'A gentle answer turns away wrath, but a harsh word stirs up anger.' Jesus Christ is 'gentle and humble in heart' (Matthew 11:29) and his followers have to learn to be like him, especially those who would lead in the church and help the wayward and those who have fallen. A self-denying attitude is important because it is when self gets involved that we are apt to lose our cool and speak in a way which is likely to provoke those we are trying to help. In work like this it doesn't matter about our feelings, nor does it matter what those we are trying to help say about us. We must not allow ourselves to be provoked or drawn into defending ourselves. We are just the Lord's servants to do what we can by his grace to minister in situations which require a spiritually-minded third party, who will keep his own personality out of it.

If the person helping take sides (though he or she must always take sides with the truth), or gets involved personally and perhaps begins to take offence the situation can actually get far worse. This is something which has often happened. Pastors or leaders have got involved in a way which has only increased the number of disputants, and brought the problem into the leadership into the bargain. The person who stands in the middle in a quarrel or a fight is quite likely to get hurt from both sides, but that doesn't matter. If he can divert the disputants from each other and gradually bring them to look at the problem in the light of Scripture, and then reconcile them to each other, he has fulfilled his responsibility and can rejoice, whatever personal pain or trouble he has had to bear. Like Paul he has to be ready to 'very gladly spend for you everything I have and expend myself as well' (2 Corinthians 12:15). True Christian love 'always protects, always trusts, always hopes, always perseveres' (1 Corinthians 13:7).

An ability to get to the heart of a matter

This is where so many of us fail, however good our intentions. It is generally by long experience that we gain this sort of discernment. What should happen is that the older leaders develop a spiritual insight and then help to develop the same in new, younger leaders. This doesn't always happen, perhaps because some leaders are proud of their abilities and always want to be the ones who put matters right. One of the reasons why leaderships should discuss problems and relational difficulties is so that all can learn together, and those with less experience can begin to see the way the more experienced handle them. At the same time this means that confidentiality must be absolute. Of course there will be situations in which only those actually involved in counselling should know the details, but not all cases are like this. It is also essential that there is input from spiritually-minded women in every case that requires this. Leadership in the sense of authority and the ministry of the Word may be male, but a woman's perspective and insight needs to be given in many cases, especially when marriage or sexual difficulties are involved.

It can often be hard to distinguish between things that are vital and things that are trivial or peripheral. In disputes and problems there are usually one or more issues that are central. If they can be cleared up then everything else falls into place easily. On the other hand a lot of time can be spent on matters which are not the real problem. People often avoid the real problem because it can be painful even to speak about it. A problem may have been long lasting and those concerned have almost buried it and don't want it resurrected. Yet it is a poison in their relationships and until the root is dug up and dealt with, it will remain to cause trouble, either as an underlying tension or breaking out from time to time, perhaps in outbursts of anger.

Action and correction has to focus on the real problem. Superficial patching up of relationships is all too easy, and many Christians and churches settle for that. The Bible is radical, it gets to the heart of our sins and self-deceptions, and leaders and peacemakers have to learn to be able to do the same. It is important to realise that more than confession and forgiveness may be needed, and leaders have to point this out. Things stolen, broken or lost by negligence need to be replaced. Positive actions to undo harm need to be taken. Those who are truly repentant will insist on doing this in any case. Generally speaking they should not be dissuaded from it even if it is going to involve them in expense and considerable inconvenience. Such actions are important both for the person who has offended and the person who was sinned against. They show the reality of repentance and satisfy the consciences of both parties. It is spiritually dangerous to short-circuit the process of making amends.

In addition where unbelieving people are involved, or the authorities, it shows that churches are not just like the world, out to cover things up as much as possible. Of course we can understand why this sometimes happens. A number of years ago a vicar fell into immorality and was suddenly moved from his ministry. An honest statement would undoubtedly have provoked a flood of lurid publicity. However the statement put out by the Bishop was as near lying as you could get. The Church was saved great embarrassment, but what was done cannot be justified and an account will have to be given to the Lord Jesus Christ. If a matter involves a criminal offence then, unless the circumstances are very exceptional, repentance means that the police will have to be informed.

Integrity and truthfulness

Surprisingly it can be difficult to be absolutely truthful in handling many problems. The reason for this is that in mediating between two sides, there is a natural desire not to antagonise either party. Moreover it is understandable that each side may want to know what you think, and want to reassure themselves that you believe their side of the story. You are under no obligation to reveal exactly what your thoughts are, and you may not be sure whose side you do believe. Unfortunately, even among Christians, people distort the truth in their own interests so much, they seem so blind to any alternative understanding of facts, that it can be almost impossible to know just what is the truth anyway.

It is no good trying to keep both sides happy with evasions and half-truths. The real peacemaker has to earn the respect of those he is trying to help. He must be seen to be even-handed, as far as possible, but not in the sense of always trying to adopt a mediating position. This is the great snare of the mediator. However things may be done in many negotiations outside the church, though to the detriment of truth and justice, the Christian is not simply concerned with balancing one side against another and coming up with a reasonable compromise. He is concerned with truth, what is right and what is wrong. He is concerned to identify sin and help the one who has sinned to repent, and the one who has been sinned against to forgive. Of course he knows that often there is fault on both sides, that often misunderstanding plays a large part in the breakdown of relationships, but he wants everything to be dealt with fully and honestly in the sight of the Lord and according to biblical principles.

For this those who would help others must be trustworthy and honourable. There is no place for the wheeler-dealer or the fixer in New Testament churches. The churches need men and women who are personally upright and honest, who have a conscience about telling the truth, who are not careless in their speech, whose, 'Yes' is 'Yes', and whose 'No' is 'No', who speak the truth in love.

Firmness

This quality is closely linked to integrity. The impression often given is that Christians are rather flabby and feeble people, easily taken in, soft-hearted like cream chocolates. Doubtless to the hard-nosed man of the world they will always seem like that, but there is rather too much truth in the caricature. Those who make peace need to be firm. When David the king had sinned we can admire the indirect way in which Nathan tackled him and got him to condemn himself. Nevertheless there came a point when Nathan had to take his courage and his life into his hands and say, 'You are the man!' (2 Samuel 12:7).

We see the same sort of firmness in the Lord Jesus Christ. While he was gentle and kind to the needy and burdened, he was outspoken and clear in his conversation and debates with the Pharisees and Jewish leaders. He was prepared to speak the truth in a way which hit home and which meant they either had to submit to it or else reject both his words and himself, as indeed they did. He was not out merely to be popular, and where he came across hypocrisy and double standards he spoke out clearly. There has to be a similar firmness with those who lead, or who try to help people in trouble today. There is still gross hypocrisy to be found among professing Christians. Sometimes we come across situations where a person has quite clearly descended to behaviour, or language, which is totally unacceptable for believers. Our Lord at times displayed a holy anger, and though we have to be very careful, for in many ways we are not like him, yet there are occasions when this is the only proper response. Church members should appreciate the love and pastoral care that their leaders have for them, but they should not be under the illusion that blatant sin or serious inconsistency is going to be overlooked and unrebuked.

Patience and love

Yet that cannot be the last word. The person who wants, by God's grace, to restore broken relationships and bring back harmony into the church must, above all else, have almost infinite patience and deep love; love for the truth, love for what is good, love for the church, love for people in spite of their sins and awkwardness, love for Christ whose church it is. We have seen this sort of love displayed by Paul in his second letter to the Corinthians. Look again at his words in 2:4, 'For I wrote to you out of great distress and anguish of heart and with many tears, not to grieve you but to let you know the depth of my love for you.' Or consider 12:14,15, 'Now I am ready to visit you for the third time, and I will not be a burden to you, because what I want is not your possessions but you. After all, children should not have to save up for their parents, but parents for their children. So I will very gladly spend for you everything I have and expend myself as well. If I love you more, will you love me less?' Or 6:11-13, 'We have spoken freely to you, Corinthians, and opened wide our hearts to you. We are not withholding our affection from you, but you are withholding yours from us. As a fair exchange—I speak as to my children—open wide your hearts also.'

The whole of that letter is an example of a Christian leader who, in a very difficult situation, longs to help the church and establish loving Christian relations, in this case between himself and his colleagues and many in the church. Those who would restore harmony need a passionate desire for the welfare of God's people and a willingness to go on and on lovingly and prayerfully giving themselves fully to bring about a successful conclusion to their task.

QUESTIONS FOR STUDY AND DISCUSSION

1. Why do Christians quarrel with each other?

2. What is necessary for forgiveness and reconciliation to take place?

3. Consider as many verses that teach us about 'peace' as you can.

4. What additional qualities can you think of that would be valuable in a peacemaker?

5. Case study: What does 2 Corinthians 7:2-16 have to teach us about restored relationships and the joy which results?

Practical steps to promote harmony

In this final chapter we consider some of the measures that will promote good relationships and harmony in a church. For this reason it naturally has a 'how-to' look about it. However harmony does not come about simply by following a set of instructions. Right attitudes, motives and desires are essential; hearts that are directed by the Holy Spirit and that pursue peace and love. This chapter is not comprehensive; in every situation you will also find the need to see what Scriptures apply particularly to those circumstances.

PREVENTATIVE MEASURES

Prevention is better than cure, and there are a number of preventative measures which wise leaders can adopt. However, members themselves are also responsible for being aware of what might harm good relationships. It is the duty of all of us 'if it is possible, as far as it depends on [us], to live at peace with everyone' (Romans 12:18).

Be alert to problems

Good leaders will not see incipient trouble round every corner, nor will they have a suspicious, prying attitude, but they will not be complacent or asleep either. They will know that it is easy for difficulties to arise, so they will keep their eyes open. If they get to know the members of the church as they ought they will also become aware of their weaknesses, and the sort of temptations they might find it hard to cope with. They will begin to realise the different backgrounds of members, their temperaments, doctrinal views, strength of conviction, and so on. They will see where members might disagree, perhaps on matters which are nothing to do with the work and witness of the church, political matters for instance. All this will help to keep them alert to areas of potential trouble.

Knowing the strengths and weaknesses of members is important from another viewpoint also. Members serve together in various activities of the church, the Sunday School, in evangelism and so on. People with very different temperaments may find it difficult to work together. This doesn't mean they can't, or shouldn't, work together, but leaders need to realise that it may not always be easy for them to do so. It is not just a question of temperament either, there are a whole range of reasons why it may be difficult for some to work together. In many cases it will actually be good for such people to have to work together, it will be part of the Lord's process of maturing them. Nevertheless leaders must be ready for any problems that might arise, and be prepared to deal with them sensitively. In some cases it will not be wise for certain people to work too closely together. A person with a timid disposition might not find it possible to work with a highly efficient, highly organised person. There is nothing wrong here. Loving one another truly in the Lord and worshipping with one heart and mind, does not mean that we are all suitable to work together in specific activities.

What has just been said has to be applied to the leadership also. There are, of course, various ways within churches in which men are appointed to leadership. We do not always realise that it is important that all on the leadership are able to work together with one another. It is not just a question of ability. A man may have leadership qualities, yet may not have yet developed the ability to work together in a team. A man may have significant differences of doctrinal and practical conviction from the other leaders which mean that he cannot really function as a leader with them. These things need to be reckoned with so as to reduce the possibility of problems and to be alert to pressure points.

Tackle difficulties in their early stages

It is not always possible to do this. Sometimes big problems arise very quickly. At other times they have been brewing secretly and no leadership could reasonably have been expected to spot them beforehand. Nevertheless in most cases difficulties do begin in a small way and gradually grow. The policy of some leaders is invariably to leave such difficulties well alone, hoping that they will die a natural death or sort themselves out without any action being taken by the leadership. Such an approach can be justified. After all it cannot be necessary for leaders to get involved every time there is a disagreement between members. If there is a difference over policy within the Sunday School it is usually better if the teachers can sort that out between them. Having said that, an eye can be kept open to see if the disagreement leads to something more, or if the Sunday School teachers have satisfactorily resolved their differences.

If problems are dealt with early on a great deal of bad feeling and hardened attitudes can be avoided. It is tragic to realise that some church splits might never have taken place if only the root causes had been spotted and dealt with early on. Leaders must be alert for the early signs of trouble, and be ready to take quick action if necessary.

Ensure there is systematic Bible teaching with practical application

All problems and difficulties are covered, at least in principle, in the Scriptures. The early churches were full of problems, and systematic Bible exposition will show the nature of these problems, how they can be avoided, and how they are to be put right. Application is not always imaginative enough, or focused adequately on the sort of problems that arise in the present day. Prepare the whole church for problems. Show how they are bound to arise in the nature of the case because of our present imperfect state. Help the congregation to be self-aware. Help people to consider themselves; to ask what sort of problems they themselves might trigger off in the church, given their own personalities, temptations and weaknesses. Make people realise how much they need to watch and pray; how subtle the devil is, how deceitful their own hearts are, how easily self affects their attitudes and even their convictions.

Show also how the Bible gives answers. Help people to realise the importance of humility and being prepared to forgive. Spell out what is needed for reconciliation to take place. Demonstrate what real repentance is, for example, from 2 Corinthians 7. Show that we must also be eager to press on, to grow in grace. Show how God uses all the ups and downs of church life to mould and mature his people. Never give people the impression there comes a time when they can slacken off and take a detached view of what is happening in the church, or of their own Christian lives. The Bible is full of examples that have a practical bearing on the lives of believers and the churches, and yet it is often not used as the resource book that it is. Leaders must ensure that the length and breadth of the Bible is brought before God's people, and that all of it plays its part in the promotion of the harmony of the church.

Encourage communication

A great many problems arise because of poor communication. People misunderstand what leaders are trying to do. Rumours about members get passed around. Half the truth gets known and this causes a problem until the other half becomes known also. People don't feel able to voice their concerns, or feel they are just put down or looked upon as trouble-makers if they do. Groups talk among themselves, but don't come out into the open and speak to leaders. Leaders act in unnecessarily secretive ways. All these are common in church life, and cause great harm. Often it is simply lack of forethought that is responsible.

The answer is to try and develop an openness and an atmosphere in which no-one feels unable to speak. This is not to deny that some things ought to remain private, that will always be the case. Nor is it right that church meetings become occasions when things that ought not to be said are brought out, or the leaders—or members—embarrassed by issues being sprung on them without warning. Nor should the same sort of thing take place in leaders' meetings either. Sometimes people avoid having to speak to another member—or leader—face to face by bringing the issue up in a meeting. Not only is this a cowardly thing to do, its natural tendency is to antagonise the other person and make what might be a potentially difficult situation worse. Even if it is something that ought to be brought into a more public forum the right thing is to speak to the individual concerned first so that he has prior warning, then as far as possible personal relationships are not jeopardised.

Leaders need to be in touch with the membership and make it easy for the members to express any concern that they might have about the church. Leaders should be able to ask members for their views. It is far better for the leaders to be able to sound out the membership and know the general opinion, and those with questions or difficulties, rather than waiting for church meetings to find out what people are thinking. If members are free to ask questions they must also expect to receive answers. Leaders ought to give reasons for proposed courses of action, and be prepared beforehand. Members must recognise that if they have cogent reasons given to them by leaders, reasons to which they can give no answer, then they should acquiesce in what the leaders propose. There is no place in church life for people just being 'agin the government' as a matter of course.

Promote good relationships in the church

This is not easy as a church grows, but it is important to do so as far as possible. In a large church there will be natural groupings into which many members fall, often those connected with some particular service or meeting. Here good relationships need to be fostered within the grouping and between it and other groupings. Opportunities need to be made for people to get to know each other. It is often the case that people who see each other twice a week in the services of the Lord's Day do not speak much with each other nor know each other very well. This is one of the benefits of more informal occasions; of house-parties and camps, of barbecues and walks and more social events. They provide times when people can mix and talk.

As churches grow it is also very easy for some people to get rather lost in the crowd, or to drift to the edge of the fellowship. No-one seems to realise they do not easily fit in to any of the groups which tend to form within the church. Leaders must do all they can to help people like this. These may be single people, or people whose partner is unconverted and who never comes to church. Sometimes they are people who seem to have many problems, sometimes they are very shy, sometimes they are constitutionally loners, sometimes they want a measure of privacy and do not always feel it natural for them to converse much with others. Thought and sensitivity is obviously necessary here. To put a solitary introvert into a group of happy extroverts—or vice versa—will probably not improve relationships!

There is a deeper and more vital matter here. We are not just out to promote friendliness, but to develop spiritual fellowship. One of the sad things is that it seems very difficult to promote spiritual conversation amongst many Christians. It is not that they talk about things that are wrong, but that often they do not rise above family matters, money matters or the weather. Friendship is fine, but fellowship is better. Talk about the family is fine, but more so when it is looked at from a biblical perspective. Consider spiritual experience; the ups and downs of the Christian life; its joys and blessings; sharing blessings for another's encouragement or matters for prayer? Why not talk about the Lord himself? When real fellowship is developed, then relationships become a different matter all together. Believers see themselves as members together in the body of Christ and the family of God; that is the real relationship we have to each other.

FIRST THINGS FIRST

On the 27th of July, 1681 the Covenanter Donald Cargill was executed. He summed up his life and ministry in these words, 'I have followed holiness. I have taught truth, and *I have been most in the main things;* not that I thought the things concerning our times little, but I thought none could do anything to purpose in God's great and public matters, till they were right in their conditions.' How right he was. Unless our spiritual condition is right before God nothing else can really be right. To keep the conditions of God's people right, personally and corporately, preachers and ministers must be most in the main things. Here are some of the priorities, or main things, that are necessary for harmony.

Keep the great truths of the gospel before the church

In Colossians 3:16 Paul says, 'Let the word of Christ dwell in you richly.' We could expand those words like this, 'Let the message that centres in Christ be at home among you richly.' 'You' is plural here. Paul is speaking about the church, which is why the word 'among' is probably more suitable than 'in', even though the word of Christ does live in the hearts of individual believers too. 'Word' refers to the message of Christ; the gospel in its fullness which centres in Jesus Christ. Paul has already been exhibiting and explaining the centrality of Christ in the two earlier chapters of this letter. For the word 'richly', the comment of N.T. Wright cannot be beaten, 'the church is to be stocked with good teaching as a palace is filled with treasures.' (N. T. Wright, *Colossians and Philemon, Tyndale New Testament Commentaries,* IVP; p.144.) The context of these words speaks of love and peace in the church (vv.12-15), and then the outflow of the word of Christ in teaching, praise and practical living together in the church (v.16,17).

What are these 'great truths of the gospel' that make up 'the word of Christ'? There is no need to think of them in any narrow way. They start with God himself, not only because it was God the Father who sent his Son, but also because the holiness and justice of God in the face of human disobedience and sin demanded the coming and saving work of Christ if salvation was going to be provided for sinners. So we are thinking of truths about the holiness and love of God; about the person of Jesus Christ, his life of obedience and death as a sacrifice; about the Holy Spirit and his work in new birth and revealing Christ. We are thinking of great themes like redemption, justification, reconciliation, adoption, and the hope of future glory; of repentance and faith, of forgiveness and cleansing, of conversion and new life, of the return of Jesus Christ and the new heavens and new earth. These are truths which the unconverted need to hear and understand, but they are also the lifeblood of a church. The greatness and glory of the Saviour is the great uniting theme which brings and keeps the members together.

This means that it is the responsibility of leaders to ensure that gospel themes are prominent in the ministry of the Word that is given. It means that there must be balance in the teaching and preaching. Balance is often achieved by preaching continuously through various books of the Bible, and there is great value in this. It would not, however, be very wise to be going through Job on Sunday mornings, Ecclesiastes on Sunday evening, and Esther at the midweek Bible Study! It is only too easy to start majoring on matters which are not of central importance. Ensuring that gospel themes are prominent in the church's ministry—not just in the Sunday services, but other aspects of the work too—keeps the Lord's people humble, thankful and full of joy for God's mercy in Christ. When we all feel we are but sinners saved by grace and indebted to God's love, divisions and unnecessary disputes seem very out of place.

Ensure that the flock are spiritually nourished

It was Milton who wrote, 'The hungry sheep look up and are not fed.' (*Lycidas,* line 123). This is a sad condition and it leads to many problems.

Those who feel they are not helped and strengthened as they ought to be by the ministry will feel dissatisfied. If this continues it will not be long before they start talking about it and the probability is that the dissatisfaction will spread. Those who do not feel they are adequately ministered to will also look around for other meetings where they feel they will receive what their souls need. This may not matter; many Christians have been helped and strengthened by Bible ministry, perhaps on a Saturday evening or at a Convention. Many pastors are not able to give the sort of ministry that the Lord enables a few to give and they will be glad when their flock are able to benefit from such ministry. They may be glad of such ministry and encouragement themselves. Nevertheless it is sad when members leave their own churches and occasionally visit other churches simply because they are not being ministered to as they ought. Eventually this leads to those who do not believe their souls are being fed leaving the church permanently.

Of course there is an added difficulty here. Many Christians have had the feeling that the grass is greener in another field, and have left their church to go to another only to find that once they got into membership, the new church had as many problems and difficulties as the first one, perhaps even more.

Another aspect is this. Where believers are not adequately fed they may not have the spiritual resources for the service which they do in the church. There have been those who have taught in Sunday School or spoken at Women's Meetings and yet their own souls have been barren and dry. There is a real danger in these circumstances of ministering simply in the energy of the flesh. The ministry of those who are not being adequately ministered to is not likely to be spiritually helpful to those who receive it. Many pastors can be in such a condition. In their case it is vital they take what steps they can to ensure they feed on the Word of God themselves.

What Christians need is an all-round ministry of the Word. Sometimes, of course, the problem is with the appetite of the Christian. He or she doesn't want anything more than a simple message repeating old and well-loved truths. But this just will not do. Living as we do in a difficult world with many demands made on faith we need a ministry which prepares us for all the temptations and trials which the modern world has for us. This is the corollary of the previous point. Moreover it is necessary that the Word of God is applied and that the element of spiritual experience is also supplied. A ministry which is all doctrine, or all application, or all experience, is unbalanced. The whole of our lives as Christians has to come under the direction and power of God's Word.

Make prayer central to church life

This should not have to be said but most wise Christians will know that they need frequently to be reminded of the importance of prayer and stirred up to pray. It is easy to assume that the church prays about everything, when its prayers may become merely a matter of habit, a routine of words which are performed in a perfunctory manner. Nor is it just a matter of much prayer; the nature and quality of the prayer that is offered is of far greater importance. Nor can prayer simply be measured by fervency, or apparent fervency. This is not a defence of cold, unfeeling prayer. It is rather a recognition that the depth, reality and spirituality of praying is not just a matter of how fervent those who pray seem to be. Raised voices or emotional whispers may be more an index of the temperament of the person praying or of what that person deems is appropriate for prayer. Above all else, prayer must be real.

Most churches have at least one meeting for prayer, though in many cases it is also shared with Bible study. That is the occasion when the church meets *as a church* to pray. There may well be other meetings for prayer, and prayer at other meetings, but there is great value in the church meeting together for prayer. It reminds everyone that the church is dependent on the Lord. It ensures that thanks are given for God's blessings. It is the time when all who come together—and God's people should be encouraged to come together like this—express their corporate involvement in all the different aspects of the church's life and ministry by their prayers. This is not to assume that everyone present will lead in prayer, or ought to lead in prayer, but all can pray as one leads, and all add their 'Amen' at appropriate points and at the end.

Christians in the past were much more likely to call special times of prayer than seems to be the case today. Yet there are many circumstances in which the natural thing for Christians ought to be to turn to prayer. The first thing that believers ought to do in times of special need is to turn to their heavenly Father. When problems or difficulties confront a church, when decisions have to be taken, when the work seems to be declining, when open sins are to be found on the part of members, where else should the church turn but to God in earnest and heartfelt prayer? When the church doesn't do this it shows that there is already a serious spiritual weakness among the members.

Some mention ought to be made of prayer in the regular services of worship. The trend seems to be for public prayer in the worship of the Lord's Day to be given a minimal place, perhaps only two or three minutes out of an hour. This is sometimes done in the interests of unbelievers who may come to the services, or for the sake of younger people, but what it says to these is that giving thanks to God, and expressing our dependence on him in prayer is not very important. If we believe that God answers prayer then we will want to pray and we will make it clear that prayer is vital. Prayers do not have to be long anyway; why is it necessary to have four hymns, or twenty songs, and only one prayer? The increase in singing and the decline of praying in public worship can only mean that congregations are more interested in enjoying themselves than they are about being serious with God, asking for his glory and blessing, and the saving of unconverted neighbours and friends.

There should be a place for prayer for everything that the church does. Leadership meetings should include prayer. This may not simply be an opening prayer. As particular matters come up on an agenda some almost cry out more for prayer than discussion. When it seems hard to get agreement, when decisions seem difficult to arrive at, when delicate matters need to be discussed, then is the time to turn to God for light and wisdom. The same is true for church meetings. The first members of the church at Jerusalem devoted themselves to prayer (Acts 2:42), in the context this refers primarily to corporate praying. This will be the case with any healthy church; in many cases a return to the priority of prayer will mean a return to a healthy and harmonious church life.

Always value grace above gifts

The Lord Jesus Christ gives gifts to the members of the churches, and these gifts need to be recognised and used for the good of the churches. But we need to be realistic about gifts and abilities. The gift of speaking effectively to others can be used for good or bad purposes. The gift of getting alongside people and making friends with them easily can be used to promote the unity of the church or to introduce dissension and form a faction with its own agenda. Those with very clear gifts are sometimes tempted to rely on their gifts rather than to rely on the Lord. Someone with a ready facility for speech may shirk the hard work of preparing a message properly because he feels able to spin out a few ideas once he's on his feet. People with great gifts can make great contributions to the life and work of a church; they can also cause great problems and not infrequently do so.

So the priority is always spirituality and godliness. It is tempting to push gifted people into positions of leadership; and also to overlook the real worth of godly people who do not have the apparent gifts of others. We have already seen how Paul emphasises Christian character when he speaks of elders and deacons. There is no substitute for this. Acts 6:3 is full of instruction at this point: "But select from among you, brethren, seven men of good reputation, full of the Spirit and of wisdom, whom we may put in charge of this task" (NASB). On the one hand the witness of these men must be good, they must be known for their Christian character. On the other they must be full of the Spirit and wisdom, which may mean, full of the Spirit who gives wisdom, or, full of wisdom by the Spirit. This is also a reminder of the importance of wisdom in the work of the Lord. This is both a gift of the Spirit (see also Isaiah 11:2; James 1:5), and also a quality that is developed by experience and learning from Jesus Christ. The fear of the Lord is the beginning of wisdom, so wisdom comes not so much from a course of study as from a reverent attitude to God, and learning from him through his Word.

Grace expresses itself in qualities like meekness, a loving spirit, a joyful approach to serving the Lord, a desire for the glory of God and the good of his people. Grace makes people self-forgetful and turns their thoughts to the interests of others (Philippians 2:4). Grace makes people like Jesus Christ. In the words of Robert Murray M'Cheyne, "It is not great gifts that God uses, so much as great likeness to Jesus." It is easy enough to pay lip service to such words, it is another thing to carry them through in practice in the church. It will mean that gifted people may be passed by when positions of leadership or service need to be filled, and those who may have a low profile in the church but are steady, dependable, spiritually-minded Christians will be preferred instead.

So it is important to develop a church in which godliness is prized above everything else. This must be done by the preaching and teaching ministry and by the attitude of the existing leaders. Those who have gifts must not only be encouraged to develop their gifts, but to develop spiritually so that their gifts do not outstrip their godliness, nor their abilities their Christian character. The priority for us all is "to grow in the grace and knowledge of our Lord and Saviour Jesus Christ" (2 Peter 3:18). Within the existing leadership it is also important to foster spiritual growth and spiritual attitudes. Times of prayer and Bible study together are an important part of the work of leadership.

Put secondary things in their place

It might be thought that this will automatically happen if first things are put first and the great truths of the gospel are emphasised. However, it is not quite as simple as that, and a conscious effort needs to be made to ensure things are kept in their proper proportion. It is often relatively trivial things that cause trouble within churches, so an eye must be kept open for these. In addition, an accumulation of small matters can lead to dissatisfaction within a congregation. Things which by themselves would not be a source of discontent can do great damage when they accumulate together. It is usually the case that there is some underlying weakness if there are a number of issues, even if small by themselves, which are causing difficulty in the church. It is likely that pastoral care is inadequate. Either the matters of concern are not known by the leaders, or they are known but the leadership for one reason or another fails to tackle them. In either case the leaders are simply not doing their work properly. This has often proved to be the case in churches. Matters are overlooked because they are deemed to be too small to bother about, whereas because they are small and secondary they could be quite easily resolved.

The point is not simply that relatively unimportant matters of doctrine need to be kept in their place. It is much more likely that practical and mundane matters get out of their place. Leaders can spend a great deal of time on things like the decoration of the building or financial matters. The great danger is that these things come to dominate leaders' meetings, when often they scarcely need to be mentioned at all. It is much better, for example, for the treasurer to have discretion over smaller items of expenditure rather than for them all to be discussed at meetings. He can just supply a list of items of expenditure so that leaders are aware of what has been spent and a proper check made, but usually there will be no need for any discussion.

Exactly the same problem can arise in church meetings. Church meeting agendas have a habit of accumulating jots and tittles of church business while weightier matters are quite overlooked. It is not just that this wastes time. It means that there is a lack of proportion at the heart of church life. Members lose a sense of priority simply because there is no discipline to ensure that the church concentrates on matters of fundamental importance.

There can be an exception to what has just been said. A matter can seem to be of relative unimportance but the circumstances and time can actually make it very important. If a member has been deeply hurt over a small issue, it has become a much larger issue and the hurt needs dealing with speedily. A case where just a small amount of money has been wrongly used or misapplied may be very serious. Watch out for cases like this, but don't allow small matters either to grow or to divert or dominate in the church.

Keep the church united

There are many appeals for unity in the New Testament. It is clearly the duty both of leaders and members to do all they can to 'keep the unity of the Spirit through the bond of peace.' The point here is this; unity must be actively pursued. It is an end in itself, even though it can also be thought of as a by-product of a healthy spiritual life together. It is necessary to watch out for things that cause division and to follow after those that promote peace and harmony. Unity arises from mutual love, and love is a fundamental priority for Christians.

It is important to watch out for anything that has the potential to harm the unity of the church. This is not to advocate a policy of peace at any price, though it is worth remembering that peace is a precious commodity, and it is worth paying a price for it. Biblical principles should not be compromised for peace, but it is a biblical principle to pursue peace; 'if it is possible, as far as it depends on you, live at peace with everyone' (Romans 12:18; see also Hebrews 12:14). It is not unusual for church members to have niggles and differences which prevent real harmony, but which could be easily dealt with if the leaders were watchful and sensitive.

Nearly every church has those on the fringe of church life, and wise leadership will try to help them and bring them further into fellowship. At the same time there may be reasons why these people remain on the touchline and these need to be understood and evaluated. Some Christians have suffered deep hurts in another church and all they want to do is to worship with the Lord's people and allow a healing process to take place. This is very understandable and should be respected. Such people should not be pressurised to join or get more involved, but be ministered to with sensitivity and love. Some people are very unsure of themselves temperamentally and they need careful encouragement which will draw them into the fellowship.

Ideally the members of a church should be active, even stretched, in their service for Christ in the church, yet not burdened or pressurised. It is often those who have nothing else to do who find time to criticise and find fault, though it is also true that those who are over-stretched often criticise those who seem to do nothing. Those who are working together with others are conscious of their own and others' weaknesses and inadequacies, but they look at these in a sympathetic way for all are involved together in the work. Once some members adopt the standpoint of bystanders or spectators there is likely to be trouble. On the other hand it is important that members are self-motivated rather than working together out of fear or guilt. By self-motivation here is meant the constraining love of Christ and the motivating power of the gospel in the heart, not acting to promote, or satisfy, or show off, self.

In keeping the church united it is important to try to develop brotherly love. The local church is a local family of the Lord's people. Before we think of leaders and followers we must remember the fundamental truth that we are all brothers and sisters in the Lord. Families may consist of people of different temperament and outlook but there is a basic natural bond which keeps them together. So in the local church emphasis must be placed on the spiritual bond of unity in Jesus Christ.

Do everything in the context of worship

The church is first and foremost a temple, a worshipping community, (1 Peter 2:5; 1 Corinthians 3:16,17). Together we offer the sacrifices of praise, prayer and thanksgiving to God (Hebrews 13:15). The direction in which we look first of all is upward and Godward. Our life together in the church, as also our responsibilities towards the world, spring out of worship, devotion and obedience to God. It is important to maintain this perspective.

This means that the glory of God must be central to everything that goes on within the church. We are not simply concerned with developing and maintaining good relationships within the church for our own peace and satisfaction; our concern is the glory of God. It is not just that harmony is better for us. The glory of God is pre-eminent, even if that sometimes means that harmony must be put on hold while we fight battles to establish the supremacy of his glory. But generally the harmony of a church promotes the glory of God, while discord and division dishonour his name. How can God be glorified, how can Christ be honoured, how can real worship take place, when believers are at loggerheads and when they refuse to take all the means that the Word of God proposes to reach godly unity?

The point is this. Everything that takes place within a church must be related to the glory of God. There is always a spiritual dimension that must be preserved. Even the most mundane of matters must be done in the context of worshipping God and giving him glory. If whole areas of church life become divorced from praise and prayer and service to God, it won't be long before trouble begins. On the other hand a church which puts a high priority on worshipping God, and whose members enjoy oneness in corporate worship, will find it much easier to work together and maintain good relationships with each other. Where God and his glory is truly central in a church, spiritual and sensitive relationships will develop.

QUESTIONS FOR STUDY AND DISCUSSION

1. How can adequate, suitable Bible teaching be given in a church?

2. How can the prayer life of a church be improved?

3. How do Christians 'grow in grace and knowledge of our Lord and Saviour Jesus Christ'?

4. What factors should unite a church?

5. Case study: In what ways may the vision of Revelation 7:9-17 inspire and help us in our church life now?

Also from Day One

A unique new
Bible devotional
with a difference

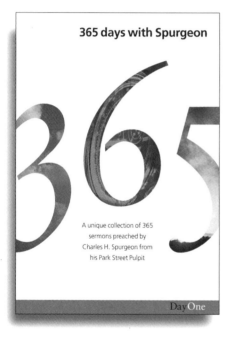

365 days with Spurgeon

*A unique daily Bible devotional
containing powerful insights from C.H.
Spurgeon's Park Street Pulpit*

384 pages
Paperback   £9.99
Casebound   £11.99

Charles Haddon Spurgeon possessed a
deep and abiding reverence for the
authority of God's Written Word (the
Bible) to the end of his days. His
application of God's eternal truths which
he found there and his recognition of how
the ensnaring affairs of daily life both
wound and affect believers, rightly places
him as a spiritual giant in the eyes of
many Christians.

In this volume, it is clear that Spurgeon
had an amazing capacity for anticipating
the daily crouching of 'sin at the door' of
every Christian, together with the biblical
antidote. Here we have absolute
confirmation that his was no late

For further information, call or write to us:

01372 728 300

flowering of Godly wisdom. Here, from the archive of Spurgeon's Park Street sermons (long before his well-known days at London's more famous Metropolitan Tabernacle) we have pearls of Biblical wisdom indeed.

What is particularly striking, however, is how incredibly appropriate they are to the ears of the contemporary Christian in need of genuine spiritual understanding. As the new millennium fast approaches, all Christians would benefit from hearing the words of such a giant of the Word. One who understood only too well the sinful nature and motives of contemporary society in search of meaning. More than that, Spurgeon provides insight into the contemporary 'worldly-wise' mind and its wearying, pressurising effect on the soul of the believing Christian living in its midst.

If it is food and medicine for the soul and wisdom for the mind which you seek, then you will find spoonfuls in these pages.

★ A unique daily Bible devotional containing powerful insights from C.H. Spurgeon's Park Street Pulpit.

★ Contains a helpful scripture index.

★ Available in case binding or paperback.

★ All editions have sewn binding and will give years of service.

ISBN 0 902 5 48 83 2 Paperback
ISBN 0 902 5 48 84 0 Casebound

In Europe: ++ 44 1372 728 300

In North America: 011 44 1372 728 300

Day One 3 Epsom Business Park Kiln Lane Epsom Surrey KT17 1JF England

email—sales@dayone.co.uk

The Beatitudes for today

John Blanchard

Large format paperback
263 pages   £7.95

Although the past thirty years have seen the publication of several excellent volumes on the Sermon on the Mount, we have lacked a full-length treatment of the Beatitudes. This excellent book attempts to fill that gap.

Reference: BEAT
ISBN 0 902548 67 0

"This is an excellent book—highly recommended for both pulpit and pew"

Our Inheritance

The Lord's Day—principles and practice

John Thackway

Paperback
32 pages   £1.25

Keeping the Lord's Day is not a straightforward matter for Christians these days. Many see it as a Cinderella, or even a mere relic of bygone days. Others are dismayed to witness so much laxness in the way believers use Sunday. Yet others do not know quite what to think—or do—when "the seventh day" comes around.

John Thackway establishes a biblical approach to the subject, and supplies practical guidance for the right use of God's day. The concise treatment will point the way to "a sabbath well spent," and should answer a number of questions that are often asked.

Reference: P13
ISBN 0 902548 72 7

For further information about these and other Day One titles, call or write to us:

01372 728 300

In Europe: ++ 44 1372 728 300

In North America: 011 44 1372 728 300

Day One 3 Epsom Business Park Kiln Lane Epsom Surrey KT17 1JF England

email—sales@dayone.co.uk   wwwdayone.co.uk

Men, Women and Authority —serving together in the church

Andrew Anderson, Series Editor

Paperback
260 pages   £7.99

This comprehensive book has been written by nine leading writers who have set out to analyse fully the issues as they are being faced by Christians today.

Reference = MWA
ISBN 0 902 548 71 9

"This book should be found on the bookshelf of all church leaders, and referred to regularly."

Our Inheritance

Only One Way

Hywel R. Jones

Andrew Anderson, Series Editor

Paperback
145 pages   £5.99

Evangelicals have always maintained that the Lord Jesus Christ is the only way to be saved—something that is now being questioned by some writers on both sides of the Atlantic.
Dr. Hywel R. Jones examines the arguments.

Reference: OOW
ISBN 0 902 548 70 0

"Important reading for all Christians who seek to take the gospel to a needy world."

Covenanter Witness

For further information about these and other Day One titles, call or write to us:

01372 728 300

In Europe: ++ 44 1372 728 300

In North America: 011 44 1372 728 300

Day One 3 Epsom Business Park Kiln Lane Epsom Surrey KT17 1JF England

eMail—sales@dayone.co.uk   wwwdayone.co.uk

Also in this series

HOMOSEXUALITY: The Straight Agenda

Andrew Anderson, Series Editor

Paperback
264 pages   £8.99

Homosexuality is one of the most controversial subjects today, both in society generally and in the denominations. It often gives rise to strong language, bitter debate and deep suspicion. This carefully researched symposium covers a wide range of issues :

★ What has been the accepted teaching of the church from the beginning?
★ How should we understand the Bible on sexuality in general and homosexuality in particular?
★ What are the causes of homosexual orientation?
★ What are the pastoral issues involved?
★ How should we respond to a homosexual in the congregation —or one who wants to become a Christian?

Reference: HOM
ISBN 0 902548 81 6

The Great Exchange: Justification by faith alone in the light of recent thought

Philip Eveson

Andrew Anderson, Series Editor

Paperback
228 pages   £7.99

"At a stroke, Philip Eveson puts the modern reader in possession of all the facts of the current dispute about the meaning of justification, and equips him or her to take part in the debate."
Evangelical Action, Australia.

Reference: TGE
ISBN 0 902548 86 7

"This piece of clear, warm theology is a priceless guide and example. Absorb, teach, rejoice in these pages! Very highly recommended."

The Banner of Truth Magazine

For further information about these and other Day One titles, call or write to us:

01372 728 300

In Europe: ++ 44 1372 728 300

In North America: 011 44 1372 728 300

Day One 3 Epsom Business Park Kiln Lane Epsom Surrey KT17 1JF England

eMail—sales@dayone.co.uk   wwwdayone.co.uk